CONFUCIUS ANALECTS
(論語)

CONFUCIUS ANALECTS

A New Translation with Annotations and Commentaries

RAYMOND K. LI

CONFUCIUS ANALECTS (論語)
A NEW TRANSLATION WITH ANNOTATIONS
AND COMMENTARIES

iUniverse books may be ordered through booksellers or by contacting:

iUniverse
1663 Liberty Drive
Bloomington, IN 47403
www.iuniverse.com
844-349-9409

ISBN: 978-1-6632-0023-5 (sc)
ISBN: 978-1-6632-0024-2 (e)

Library of Congress Control Number: 2020916759

Print information available on the last page.

iUniverse rev. date: 10/15/2020

CONTENTS

FOREWORD

There is a wealth of knowledge, insights and wisdom in the Chinese literature based on the teachings of Confucius. Raymond's translation and his commentaries enabled many among us who are not proficient in Chinese to be able to appreciate these historical gems. This is a great contribution. Going through the Analects is like a journey on learning how one can develop critical, righteous, and caring perspectives in life.

Hau L. Lee,
The Thoma Professor of Operations, Information and Technology, Stanford University.

Although the Analects has been one of the most influential books in China for the last 2,500 years, many of the English translations of this book have been incomprehensible. Raymond Li's book provides the English-speaking world with a very easy-to-read translation in simple language that has also been adopted to the modern context. Raymond has now made this great classic much more accessible to the general English-speaking public. Hopefully, his book will facilitate greater understanding between the West and the East.

Mitchell W. Hedstrom,
Greenwich, Connecticut, USA.

I love reading this book. I know the Chinese language but not enough to understand ancient Chinese texts. This book does a great job in translating and annotating a Chinese classic so that common readers like myself can easily understand an important Chinese philosophy. I am going to read this book to my eight-year old daughter at bedtime.

Ee Wah Lim,
New York, USA.

Li's translation of the Analects is very refreshing. His interpretation of the teachings of Confucius is truly insightful. I like particularly the introduction of the backgrounds of Confucius' disciples, which makes the master's words even more meaningful.

Yiu Kuen Tse,
Professor of Economics,
Singapore Management University.

PREFACE

Confucius (also known as Kong Qiu, 孔丘, and Kong Zhong Ni, 孔仲尼, 551–479 BC) was a prominent, if not the most influential, philosopher of China. He was revered as a saint by many Chinese. His teachings have been fundamental to Chinese civilization and culture for more than two and half millennia. During his early life, he tried to become a government official in his motherland, the state of Lu (魯國) and other feudal states during the Spring-Autumn Period (around 770 to 400 BC) of China so that he could apply his ideology. He was not quite successful in that endeavor because many states were decadent, and their governments were corrupt. Most rulers rejected his ideas.

The disappointed Confucius began to teach disciples during the latter part of his life. It was said that he educated as many as three thousand students from all walks of life and nurtured ten remarkable disciples who later preached his ideology, which has since been developed into a prominent philosophy, Confucianism. Wikipedia. org has a section on the details of the life of Confucius. The reader can refer to articles on Wikipedia.org for more information about this great man.

The Analects was written and compiled by Confucius's disciples after his death. It documented his conversations with his disciples and with other relevant characters and the dialogues among his disciples. These conversations highlighted key doctrines of Confucianism and cover a wide range of topics on education, self-cultivation, morality, ethics, society, social norms, government, law and order, politics, public service careers, music, poetry, and so on.

Many salient teachings of *The Analects* are still applicable to the modern world. *The Analects* had twenty chapters. The title of each chapter was taken from the first few words of the first sentence of the first conversation in the chapter and had little relevance to the subject matter of the chapter. Each chapter contains three to forty-five paragraphs, and the sequence numbers are shown in the chapter of the main text.

Different from many translations, this new translation has deployed plain and colloquial English, a simple writing style, and modern context to facilitate comprehension by common readers. This translation has also accurately preserved the ideas and tone of the original text. This book also contains annotations and explanations associated with each paragraph of *The Analects*, where necessary, to further explain the background history, circumstances, logic of the conversation, and the characters involved in the conversation. They are shown below the paragraph and labeled with the same sequence number of the paragraph plus a suffix "a."

For brevity, the original text of *The Analects* in Chinese is not included in this translation. This text is widely available in the public domain, and the interested reader can download it from the internet or buy a book on *The Analects* with Chinese text (see reference 1). In this translation, the names of characters in the original text are transcribed phonetically. Since the same transcribed name in English may refer to two different persons, to avoid confusion, this translation appends the names in Chinese characters to the transcribed names.

This book is not fiction or nonfiction. This book is also not an academic piece, although it is written with academic rigor. The primary objective of this book is to present valuable teachings for self-cultivation to common readers. The secondary objective is to expound on Confucius's ideology regarding political philosophy and public service.

The best way to get the benefit of self-cultivation is to read this book slowly at a pace of a few paragraphs at a time and then pause, ponder, and continue with a few more paragraphs later. Upon reading a paragraph, the reader should think critically about the implications of the teaching of the paragraph to his or her life, family, friends, work, society, and the world at large, and most importantly whether he or she agrees or disagrees with the teaching. It is important to extract the teachings out of ancient context and adapt them to modern life. For example, superiors, bosses, authorities, leaders of society, and rulers of governments are substitutes for the notion of "kings" mentioned repeatedly in *The Analects*.

The reader is encouraged to jot down comments and notes in the space provided under each paragraph. If the reader agrees with the teaching, he or she should strive to practice it in the future. In a few months, the reader will reap the substantial benefits of self-cultivation.

CHAPTER 1

LEARNING (學而)

1 Confucius said, "Reviewing and practicing regularly what you have learned is a pleasure indeed, isn't it? When friends and comrades visit you from afar, you would be glad indeed, would you not? If people do not reckon you and you do not blame them and get upset, you are a Jun Zi indeed, are you not?"

1a The common native name of Confucius is Kong Zi (孔子, 551–479 BC, the founder of Confucianism, the dominant philosophy in ancient China). The word *Zi* in ancient China means a courteous address of "mister" or "master" (see endnote 1).

The noun *Jun Zi* (君子) is used in Chinese scholarly texts to mean a gentleman, a person of noble character, a prominent and respectable person in society, or a person who upholds virtuous principles (see endnote 2).

2 You Zi said, "It is rare to find a person who is filial to his parents, respectful and obedient to his elder brothers, and yet repugnant to his seniors and rebellious to the authority. It is impossible to find a person who is not rebellious but tends to revolt against the authority. A Jun Zi should focus on his basic moral principles. Once these are established and committed, other principles of life follow."

2a You Zi (有子, also known as You Ruo有若, born around 518 BC) was a student of Confucius. Filial piety and fraternal respect for elder brothers are the two primary moral principles of Confucianism. In the Chinese text, the word *Tao* (道) is mentioned. This word has different meanings under different schools of philosophy. For Taoists, this means the way of nature that governs all phenomena in the sky and on earth (see reference 2). For Confucians, this word has a narrower meaning, which refers to humaneness and all the fundamental principles for human behavior and government.

3 Confucius said, "Flowery words and fawning manners seldom are Ren."

3a The word *Ren* (仁) in Confucianism embodies all core virtues of humanity, including love. It can be translated into "humaneness" and "benevolence" as a proxy. Since it cannot be translated precisely to a single English word, the Chinese pronunciation *Ren* is used here and in the following translation (see endnote 3).

4 Zheng Zi said, "I examine my own behavior many (at least three) times a day and ask, 'Was I loyal to my boss?,' 'Was I honest to my friends?,' and 'Have I reviewed and practiced what my teacher has taught?'"

4a Zheng Zi (曾子, also known as Zheng Shen曾参, born 505 BC) was a prominent disciple of Confucius, known for his filial piety. He was the author of *The Book of Great Learning* (大學) (see endnote 4 and reference 4).

5 Confucius said, "If you are the governor of a state that owns a thousand chariots, you should manage its affairs seriously and respectfully, keep your promises, practice austerity, love your staff, and direct your people expediently."

5a During the Spring-Autumn Period (around 770 to 400 BC) of China, a chariot was pulled by four horses and carried three soldiers. In an army formation, a chariot was surrounded and supported by one hundred soldiers. A thousand chariots therefore required one hundred thousand soldiers. A state that owned one hundred thousand soldiers was a decent-sized but not a large sovereign (see endnote 5).

6 Confucius said, "A young person should be filial to parents at home, respectful and obedient to teachers and seniors outside. He should be conscientious with his deeds and words. He should love others and practice Ren. After these, he should apply his spare energy to study the classics."

6a The classics here mean *The Ancient Book of Poetry, The Book of History, The Book of Rites, The Book of Changes,* and so on. Ren (仁) in Confucianism embodies all core virtues of humanity, including love. It can be translated into "humaneness" and "benevolence" as a proxy (see endnote 6).

7 Zi Xia said, "If a person respects and follows virtuous sages, renounces worldly temptations, supports his parents gratefully and unconditionally, serves his king [boss] wholeheartedly, keeps his words when dealing with friends, we can say that he is already a learned person even though he has not received any formal education."

7a Zi Xia (子夏, born 507 BC) was a disciple of Confucius and later became an official of the state of Wei (魏國). Some scholars also interpret the phrase "renounces worldly temptations" as "denies sexual appeals." The interpretation in this book seems more appropriate because "sexual appeals" are more specific whereas "worldly temptations" are more general and include sexual appeals.

8 Confucius said, "A Jun Zi must be passionately committed to his principles; else he will lose his dignity and his knowledge will not be firm. He should uphold loyalty and honor. He should not befriend people of lower moral character than his. He should not be afraid of correcting his own mistakes."

8a Jun Zi (君子) is a gentleman, a person of noble character, a prominent and respectable person in society, or a person who upholds virtuous principles.

9 Zheng Zi said, "If a ruler handles the funeral of his parents respectfully and pays homage to his ancestors, a virtuous society will gradually be developed."

9a Since Confucius and Zheng Zi regarded filial piety to be the basis of all other virtues, the above sentence means that the ruler should set an example for his people by displaying filial behavior. His people will then emulate him, and so a virtuous society will ensue.

10 Zi Qin asked Zi Gong, "Our teacher knew the internal politics of every country he has visited. Did he beg for such information? Or was it given to him without his request?" Zi Gong replied, "Our teacher got such information because people liked his mild, kind, respectful, discreet, and modest personality. His way of getting confidential information is quite unique."

10a Some scholars think that Zi Qin (子禽, also known as Chen Kang 陈亢, born around 511 BC) was a student of Confucius, while other scholars think he was not. He later became an official of the state of Wey (衛國).

Zi Gong (子貢, also known as Duan Mu Ci 端木賜, born around 520 BC) was one of the top ten disciples of Confucius. He later became the prime minister of the states of Lu (魯國) and Wey

(衛國). He also made a fortune in business and was the wealthiest disciple of Confucius. He advocated making money through propriety, honesty, and trust. His eloquence was also well known. After Confucius's death, Zi Gong observed six years of mourning vigil to show his deep respect for Confucius.

11 Confucius said, "When your father is alive, you observe his ideals. After his death, you note his past deeds. If you follow his righteous ideals and ways over a long time, you are indeed filial and pious."

11a A direct translation of the last sentence would be: "If you follow his righteous ideals and ways over three years, you are indeed filial and pious." Since ancient Chinese used "three years" to describe a long time, the sentence did not mean exactly three years but a long time. Otherwise, the reader could misunderstand that the respect for one's parents needs to last for three years only.

12 You Zi said, "In the practice of courteous etiquette, customary rites, and discipline (Li禮), harmony is the key. This shows the wisdom of our ancient saintly kings. However, it is not feasible to just rely on the desire for harmony as a basis to handle all matters, big or small. It is not practical to achieve harmony with the expectation that it is a common desire and knowledge, and to put aside etiquette, customary rites, regulations, and discipline (Li)."

12a You Zi (有子, also known as You Ruo有若, born around 518 BC) was a student of Confucius.

The word *Li* (禮) in Confucianism and in the Chinese language in general has many meanings. In ancient times, it referred to rites, rituals, ceremonies, protocols in courts and government, discipline, regulations, laws and order, respect, courtesy, and etiquette in daily life; in modern times, it refers to respect, etiquette, courtesy, presents, and gifts. Li (禮) includes a set of social norms that are motivated by the inner conscience of people and entrenched in the culture rather than externally imposed by the government through decrees and legislation. In the context of *The Analects*, this word has the former meaning (see endnote 7).

Ancient saintly kings refer to Yao (堯, 2356–2255 BC), Shun (舜, 2294–2184 BC), the Great Yu of Xia Dynasty (禹, around 2237–2139 BC), Tang of Shang Dynasty (湯, 1670–1587 BC), King Wen of the Zhou Dynasty (周文王, 1152–1056 BC), and King Wu of the Zhou Dynasty (周武王, died 1043 BC).

13 You Zi said, "If trust is built upon mutual respect for righteousness and honor (Yi), promises will be kept. If you show respect for people in line with proper etiquette (Li), you can avoid embarrassment and shame. If you rely on trustworthy people, you will be in control."

13a The original text mentioned the word *Yi* (義). It is translated here to be "righteousness" and "honor." In Confucianism, this word has a broader meaning, which is the set of moral standards in compliance with Li (禮) and in pursuance of Ren (仁).

14 Confucius said, "A Jun Zi does not crave for gluttonous satisfaction when he eats or for comfort where he lives. He is prompt in actions and cautious in speech. He rectifies his flaws under the guidance of virtuous masters. As such, he is indeed an earnest learner."

14a In Chinese culture, learning includes moral and spiritual training, self-refinement, and cultivation of wisdom as well as the acquisition of knowledge and skills. Therefore, the word *learner* should not be interpreted narrowly as a student in pursuit of knowledge and skills only. Otherwise, the above words of Confucius seem illogical.

15 Zi Gong asked Confucius, "If one is poor but does not fawn, or if one is rich but does not flaunt, is he good enough?" Confucius replied, "That is good enough. However, that is not as good as being poor but contented or being rich but observant to Li (禮)." Zi Gong then asked, "*The Book of Poetry* has a quote: 'Refining yourself like cutting, mixing, carving, and polishing.' Does this refer to what you just said?" Confucius replied, "Good guy, I can now start teaching you *The Book of Poetry*! You can infer from what I have said to what I have yet to teach you."

15a As explained above, the word *Li* (禮) in Confucianism and in the Chinese language in general has many meanings. In ancient times, it referred to rites, rituals in ceremonies, protocols in courts and government, discipline, regulations, laws and order, respect, courtesy, and etiquette in daily life; in modern times, it refers to respect, etiquette, courtesy, presents, and gifts. In the context of this paragraph, this word has the ancient meaning.

The Book of Poetry (詩經) was compiled during the Zhou Dynasty (周朝, around 1043 to 256 BC) as a collection of national folk songs (國風), royal paeans (大雅), royal poems (小雅), and hymns (頌). National folk songs were a collection of folk songs of various states. Royal paeans were chanted in formal occasions by the emperor and princes. Royal poems were recited in feasts. Hymns were sung during ceremonies of sacrifice in temples (see endnote 6).

16 Confucius said, "I am not concerned that other people do not understand me. I worry that I do not understand other people."

CHAPTER 2

GOVERN (為政)

1 Confucius said, "If you govern a country by upholding moral and ethical principles, your position will be as secure as the North Star, which is surrounded and adored by other stars."

1a The North Star is also known nowadays as the Polaris or the Little Dipper. Its position in the sky is very stable. Therefore, ancient Chinese considered it to be a symbol of the emperor in command of other surrounding stars. During the Spring-Autumn Period, there was a philosophy school that advocated the institution of harsh laws to rule a country. Confucius objected to this approach. Instead, he preached the fostering of Li (禮), moral and ethical principles (De 德) (see paragraph 3 and endnote 8).

2 Confucius said, "*The Book of Poetry* has three hundred verses. They can be summarized with one phrase: purity of mind."

2a *The Book of Poetry* (詩經) was compiled during the Zhou Dynasty (周朝, around 1043 to 256 BC) as a collection of national folk songs (國風), royal paeans (大雅), royal poems (小雅), and hymns (頌).

3 Confucius said, "If you use laws and regulations to guide and rule your people, and punishment to enforce their compliance, they will be decadent and shameless because they are motivated just by their desire for avoidance of punishment. If you foster moral and ethical principles, and regulate your people with Li (禮), they will not only have their sense of shame but will also be compliant."

3a This was the central theme of Confucius's political philosophy. This was reiterated by later disciples such as Mencius (孟子). This is also relevant to modern societies that have a common flaw: overreliance on the legal system and a deficiency of moral and ethical education.

4 Confucius said, "Since the age of fifteen, I have devoted myself to learning; since thirty, I have established my goals and stance in society; since forty, I have been able to resist temptations; at the age of fifty, I knew my destined mission in life; since sixty, I have been able to distinguish right or wrong from what I hear; since seventy, I have been able to do freely whatever I want without breaking any rules and norms."

4a This sentence has been quoted frequently by Chinese people throughout history. It establishes the different stages of spiritual and intellectual development of a Jun Zi.

5 Meng Yi Zi asked Confucius about filial piety. Confucius said, "Do not violate Li (禮)." Shortly afterward, Fan Chi arrived, and Confucius told him, "Meng asked me about filial piety, and I replied, 'Do not violate Li.'" Fan Chi asked, "What does that mean?" Confucius said, "When your parents are alive, you serve them according to Li; when they are dead, you bury them and organize a funeral ceremony in remembrance of them according to Li."

5a Meng Yi Zi (孟懿子, 518–481 BC) was a descendant of a noble family and an official of the state of Lu (魯國).

Fan Chi (樊遲, born about 505 BC) was a prominent disciple of Confucius.

The word *Li* (禮) referred to rites, rituals in ceremonies, protocols in courts and government, discipline, regulations, laws and order, respect, courtesy, and etiquette in daily life. Li (禮) embodied a set of social norms that are motivated by the inner conscience of people and entrenched in the culture rather than externally imposed by the government through decrees and legislation.

6 Meng Wu Bo asked Confucius about filial piety. Confucius replied, "[You must appreciate that] parents are very worried when their children get sick."

6a Meng Wu Bo (孟武伯, the son of Meng Yi Zi孟懿子, ancestor of Mencius) was a minister of the state of Lu (魯國). The original Chinese text was interpreted by scholars in two ways. The above is the first way. The second interpretation is: "You should get very worried when your parents get sick." Meng Wu Bo was known to be a spoiled and decadent person and an alcoholic. When he asked about filial piety, Confucius did not reprimand Meng for his bad behaviors. Instead, he reminded Meng of his parents' love of him and their worry and anxiety when he got sick. He should therefore return the same love to his parents. Therefore, the first interpretation is more appropriate.

7 Zi You asked about filial piety. Confucius said, "Most people nowadays think that filial piety is just about feeding your old parents. Even dogs and horses are fed by people. If you do not respect your parents, how do you differentiate feeding your parents from feeding dogs and horses?"

7a Zi You (子游, also known as Yan Yan言偃, 506–443 BC) was a prominent disciple of Confucius. This is an important lesson to all children. Filial piety comes from the heart. Only material support of and gifts to parents are not enough.

8 Zi Xia asked about filial piety. Confucius said, "The most difficult behavior is to show respectful, obedient, and amiable manners. If the young person handles chores on behalf of seniors when there is a need, or if seniors are treated with food and wine when available, are such acts enough to show filial piety according to Zheng Zi? [Of course not!]"

8a Zi Xia (子夏, born 507 BC) was a disciple of Confucius and later became an official of the state of Wei (魏國).

Zheng Zi (曾子, also known as Zheng Shen曾參, born 505 BC) was a prominent disciple of Confucius, known for his filial piety. He was the author of *The Book of Great Learning* (大學).

9 Confucius said, "Whenever I talked to Yan Hui, he kept quiet all day, not raising any question or objection, as if he was stupid. I later observed his good behaviors and words in private and discovered that he is not stupid at all."

9a Yan Hui (颜回, also known as Yan Yuan顏淵, 521–481 BC) was the best disciple of Confucius. Confucius held him in the highest regard among his disciples.

10 Confucius said, "You observe the motivation of a person's behavior and words, the approach and directions he follows, and his mental and emotional conditions. What can he hide? What can he hide?"

11 Confucius said, "If you can get new discovery and ideas from the review of past knowledge, such new discovery can then be your teacher."

12 Confucius said, "A Jun Zi should not be just an apparatus."

12a A Jun Zi (君子) is a gentleman, a person of noble character, a prominent and respectable person in society, or a person who upholds virtuous principles. "An apparatus" has a figurative meaning in this sentence. It refers to a tool that serves just one purpose. It also refers to a person who can be hired and disposed of by a master. A person who has just a body but no virtuous conscience is like an apparatus.

13 Zi Gong asked about the qualification of being a Jun Zi. Confucius said, "A Jun Zi takes action in accordance with what he has yet to say and then talks about it after the action."

13a This also implies doing good work proactively. A Jun Zi takes real actions and avoids phony promises.

14 Confucius said, "A Jun Zi conforms but does not collude, whereas a Xiao Ren (小人) colludes but does not conform."

14a A Xiao Ren (小人) is a person with the opposite characteristics of a Jun Zi. A Xiao Ren is, for example, mean, wicked, cruel, dumb, and/or lacking in virtues. The term *Xiao Ren* appears repeatedly in the text of *The Analects*. Although a Jun Zi is a team player, he does not join gangs. On the contrary, a Xiao Ren does the opposite (see endnote 9).

15 Confucius said, "Learning from books without critical thinking results in confusion. Thinking vacuously without learning from books is perilous."

15a This sentence emphasizes the need for both critical thinking and learning from books.

16 Confucius said, "It is indeed harmful to be obsessed with extremist theories."

16a Under Confucianism, both the excessive and inadequate extremes of any phenomenon are inappropriate. An extremist theory must be examined for its truth and rejected if found untrue. This is the essence of *The Doctrine of the Mean* (中庸) (see paragraph 29a of Chapter 6, endnote 14 and reference 10).

17 Confucius said, "You, do you know what I have taught you? Really understanding what you claim to know and admitting what you do not know is wisdom."

17a The first word "You" was the nickname of Confucius's disciple, Zi Lu (子路, 542–480 BC), who was also called Zhong You (仲由). This sentence teaches honesty and humility in learning. One should not pretend to know what he does not know. The humility to admit ignorance on a subject will motivate one to explore it. If one is pretentious and arrogant, one cannot learn much.

18 Zi Zhang asked about how to get an official appointment. Confucius said, "Listen to more opinions from other people and put aside those you are skeptical of. You then discuss the remainder cautiously. In this way, you will make fewer mistakes. Watch more behaviors of other people and put aside those you are skeptical of. You then follow the remainder cautiously. In this way, you will have fewer regrets. Since you talk with fewer mistakes and act with fewer regrets, your appointment is ascertained."

18a Zi Zhang (子張, 503–447 BC) was a disciple of Confucius.

19 Ai Gong asked, "What should I do to earn loyalty and approval from my people?" Confucius respectfully replied, "If you appoint and promote righteous persons as ministers and set aside wicked and crooked candidates, your people will be loyal to you. If, on the other hand, you appoint and promote wicked and crooked persons as ministers and set aside righteous candidates, your people will not be loyal to you."

19a Ai Gong (哀公) was the duke of Lu (魯國) from 494 to 468 BC (see endnote 10).

20 Ji Kang Zi asked, "How do I make my people respectful, loyal, and industrious?" Confucius replied, "If you treat your people with dignity, they will respect you. If you show piety to your parents and kindness to children and subordinates, your people will be loyal to you. If you promote the righteous and teach the incompetent, your people will be industrious."

20a Ji Kang Zi (季康子, died 468 BC) was the prime minister of the state of Lu (魯國) during the reign of Ai Gong (哀公) and was the most powerful official.

21 Somebody asked Confucius, "Why don't you enter politics and become a government official?" Confucius replied, "*The Book of History* stated, 'Filial piety to your parents and fraternal love of your brothers.' Such virtues will influence the society. This is already political involvement. Why must one become a government official?"

21a *The Book of History* (書, also known as *The Book of Documents, Classic of History, Shangshu* 尚書, and *Shu Jing* 書經) is one of the five classics of ancient Chinese literature. It covers the political history of China from the Yao (堯) and Shun (舜) periods (about 2336–2184 BC), to the Great Yu of Xia Dynasty (禹, around

2237–2139 BC) and to the Spring-Autumn Period (春秋, about 800–500 BC). It recorded the constitution, governance counsel, admonition, decree, declaration of war, and mandates given by kings and deliberated in courts. The Yao and Shun periods were considered utopian by later scholars. This book therefore teaches rulers and officials how to be benevolent and good rulers (see reference 8).

22 Confucius said, "If a person has no credibility, what can he do? He is like a big truck without clamps for yoking the ox or a small carriage without clamps for yoking the horse. How can it run?"

23 Zi Zhang asked, "Can we predict the Li system ten generations from now?" Confucius replied, "The Yan Dynasty inherited the Li system from the Xia Dynasty with known minor amendments. The Zhou Dynasty then inherited the Li system from the Yan Dynasty with also known minor amendments. We can predict the shape of it even after many generations from the current Zhou Dynasty."

23a The Xia Dynasty (夏朝) was from about 2070 to 1766 BC. The Yan Dynasty (殷朝) was also called the Shang Dynasty (商朝) and was from about 1766 to 1046 BC. The Zhou Dynasty (周朝) was from about 1046 to 256 BC.

Zi Zhang (子張, 503–447 BC) was a disciple of Confucius.

The Li (禮) system during those times was a collection of rites, rituals in ceremonies, protocols in courts and government, discipline, regulations, laws and order, respect, courtesy, and etiquette in daily life.

24 Confucius said, "Paying homage to another person's ancestors is flattery. Being aloof from a righteous obligation is cowardice."

24a Under the Li system of the Zhou Dynasty, a person was not supposed to pay homage to another person's ancestors.

CHAPTER 3

EIGHT LINES (八佾)

1 Confucius criticized Ji Ping Zi saying, "He entertains with eight lines of dancers in his courtyard. Since he allows such overt violation of the Li, what else does he not allow?"

1a Ji Ping Zi (季平子, also known as Ji Sun Si季孫氏, died 505 BC) was a descendant of a powerful family of the state of Lu (魯國) and its prime minister. According to the Zhou Li (周禮), only the imperial emperor of the Zhou Dynasty could entertain with a dance troupe of sixty-four dancers arranged in eight lines of eight dancers each. The other kings could entertain with forty-eight dancers arranged in six lines. Ministers of feudal states could entertain with thirty-two dancers arranged in four lines. Since Ji was only a minister in a feudal state, he was supposed to entertain with only four lines of dancers. By entertaining with eight lines, Ji violated the Li at that time, showing his disrespect for the imperial emperor and his own king and blatant abuse of his power. Therefore, Confucius criticized him. Confucius was an ardent defender of Li.

2 The three dominant families of the state of Lu sang the royal paeans in *The Book of Poetry* when they offered sacrifices during a ceremony of ancestral worship. Confucius said, "There are two verses of the royal paeans that say: 'Feudal kings standing by, while

the imperial emperor solemnly offers the sacrifice.' How dare the three families sing the royal paeans in their temples?"

2a The three dominant families of the state of Lu (魯國) were the descendants of Meng Sun Si (孟孫氏), Su Sun Si (叔孫氏), and Ji Sun Si (季孫氏). They dominated the government of the state of Lu. According to Zhou Li (周禮), only the imperial emperor of Zhou could sing royal paeans and hymns during ancestral ceremonies. Since members of these families were just ministers of a feudal state, they did not have the privilege of singing royal paeans. Their behavior showed their hubris and disrespect for the hierarchy.

3 Confucius said, "Would a person without the virtue of Ren practice Li? Would a person without the virtue of Ren appreciate music?"

3a The word *Ren* (仁) in Confucianism embodies all core virtues of humanity, including love. It can be translated into "humaneness" and "benevolence" as a proxy. Since it cannot be translated precisely to a single English word, the transcription of the Chinese word *Ren* is used here and in the following paragraphs (see endnote 3).

4 Lim Fang asked about the essence of Li. Confucius said, "This is a big question. Regarding the practice of Li, frugality is preferred to extravagance. Regarding funeral ceremonies, sorrowful mourning is more important than elaborate rituals."

4a Lim Fang (林放) was not a disciple of Confucius.

The rituals of Zhou Li (周禮) were elaborate, cumbersome, and often cosmetic. Therefore, Confucius pointed out that the essence was the mind rather than superficial appearance.

5 Confucius said, "Although barbaric tribes in the north and east territories have their kings, they are not as civilized as all the states in the central region, which do not even have kings."

5a In ancient China, only those states in the central region were considered part of greater China. Tribes in the north and east were considered barbarians.

6 The family Ji Si planned to hold a ceremony to worship Tai Shan. Confucius asked Zi You, "Can you prevent it from happening?" Zi You replied, "No, I cannot." Confucius then exclaimed, "My goodness! Is the God of Tai Shan inferior to Lim Fang?"

6a Ji Si （季氏） was one of the three dominant families of the state of Lu （魯國）, Confucius's motherland. In Confucius's era, there was a tradition of worshipping the gods of mountains. However, according to Zhou Li （周禮）, only the imperial emperor of the Zhou Dynasty （周朝） had the right to pay homage to the God of Tai Shan, the tallest mountain in central China at that time. The mountain Tai Shan symbolized the imperial emperor. Since the descendant of the Ji Si family was just a minister of the feudal state of Lu （魯國）, his political status was much lower than the imperial emperor. Holding a ceremony to worship Tai Shan was then a blatant violation of Zhou Li and disregard of the imperial emperor.

Zi You （子有, also known as Ran You, 冉有, Ran Qiu, 冉求 born in 522 BC) was the chief of staff of the Ji Si family and a disciple of Confucius. Therefore, Confucius asked him whether he could persuade his boss to drop the plan.

Lim Fang （林放） was an ordinary person. Since the God of Tai Shan was revered to symbolize righteousness, graciousness, and virtuous, Confucius lamented that Ji Si's action was a big insult to the God of Tai Shan.

7 Confucius said, "A Jun Zi should not engage in any fight. If, however, a fight is unavoidable, it should be in the form of a shooting match. Both sides should politely bow to each other before the match. After the match is over, they should toast drinks. This is how a Jun Zi would fight."

7a Confucius advocated the Olympic spirit two thousand years ago! A Jun Zi (君子) is a gentleman, a person of noble character, a prominent and respectable person in society, or a person who upholds virtuous principles.

8 Zi Xia asked, "What is the deep meaning of the verses: 'With sweet smiles so innocent; Charming eyes so seductive; A touch of rouge on fair skin'?" Confucius said, "You paint on a white background." Zi Xia then asked, "Do you mean that Li follows Ren?" Confucius said, "You can read my mind. I can now teach you *The Book of Poetry.*"

8a Zi Xia (子夏, born 507 BC) was a disciple of Confucius and later became an official of the state of Wei (魏國). The first two verses came from *The Book of Poetry.* The last verse had no origin. These verses used a girl's beauty as an analogy for the virtue of a Jun Zi. It starts with innocence and purity like the fair face of the girl. The sweet smile, charming eyes, and red cheeks are additional virtues on top of innocence and purity. Therefore, Confucius replied, "You paint on a white background." The white background symbolizes purity, the foundation of Ren (仁). Li (禮), like painting, is learned afterward (see endnote 6).

9 Confucius said, "I can talk a bit about the Li (禮) of the Xia Dynasty. However, the descendants Ji of the Xia Dynasty have not maintained a complete archive of it. I can also talk a bit about the Li (禮) of the Shang Dynasty. Their descendants, Song, also have not maintained a complete archive of it. Therefore, we are left with

incomplete documentation. If the documentation is complete, we can then study them."

9a The small state Ji (杞) descended from the Xia Dynasty (夏朝, 2070–1766 BC). Another small state, Song (宋), descended from the Shang Dynasty (商朝, 1766–1046 BC). It was a hegemon during the early part of the Spring-Autumn Period.

10 Confucius said, "After the imperial emperor of Zhou toasts the first wine to his ancestors, I do not want to watch the rest."

10a According to the Zhou Li (周禮), the imperial emperor of Zhou had to host a very elaborate ceremony for the worship of ancestors every five years. This ceremony was held in the Imperial Temple. In this ceremony, the emperor had to toast wine to ancestors one by one, starting from the founding fathers, Emperor Wen (周文王) and Wu (周武王). The Zhou Dynasty was most glorious and benevolent during the days of its founding fathers and had since deteriorated. Therefore, Confucius lamented that only the earliest founding fathers deserved a toast, whereas later ancestors did not.

11 Somebody asked Confucius about the rationale of the rituals in the ceremony of Imperial Worship of Ancestors. Confucius replied by showing his hand. "I don't know. Those who know the rationale should know the affairs of the entire empire as if they are all in one hand."

11a According to Zhou Li (周禮), only the imperial emperor and officials of the Zhou Dynasty could participate in the Imperial Worship of Ancestors. Since Confucius had been just an official of the feudal state of Lu (魯國) and some other smaller feudal states, his status was not high enough to participate in this ceremony. As a matter of courtesy and modesty, he therefore declined to comment on the rationale of this ceremony. The lesson: "Do not criticize when you are an outsider, you do not know enough, or you have no role in the matter."

12 There was a common saying that one should worship his ancestors as if the ancestors were present, and one should worship a god as if the god is present. Confucius said, "If my heart is not in the worship, it is equivalent to not worshipping at all."

12a Confucius criticized superficial and routine practices of worship ceremonies.

13 Huang Sun Jia asked, "There is a common proverb saying that, instead of adoring the god in the southwest, one would rather adore the god of the kitchen. What does it mean?" Confucius replied, "Not so. Once you have offended the Sky (God), praying is futile."

13a Huang Sun Jia (王孫賈, born around 502 BC) was a powerful minister of the small feudal state of Wey (衛國) during the reign of Wey Ling Gong (衛靈公, 540–493 BC), the duke of Wey (衛國). Confucius was also a minister of the state of Wey at one point in time. Huang intended to persuade Confucius to join his gang and undermine the king. Huang asked this subtle question by citing a common proverb at that time. The god in the southwest was believed to be the god who oversaw proper behaviors of people. The god of the kitchen provided food and nourishment to people. (In ancient times, the southwest corner of a house was most important and housed the master of a home. The kitchen was usually located in the opposite corner of the house). This proverb subtly meant that people should be pragmatic; food and fortune were more important than honor and propriety. Huang cited this proverb to subtly convey the message that he was the most powerful person in the government and could provide a good career to Confucius if he joined Huang's gang. Confucius then subtly rejected him by saying that propriety and righteousness were more important than food.

14 Confucius said, "Zhou Li was derived from the previous two dynasties: Xia and Shang. Since it is so elaborate and fascinating, I endorse Zhou Li."

14a Xia (夏朝) and Shang (商朝) were the two preceding dynasties of Zhou (周朝). Hence, Zhou Li (周禮) was an enhanced version of the previous Li.

15 Confucius entered the Imperial Temple and asked many questions related to it. Somebody complained, "Does this son of our neighboring state know courtesy?" Upon hearing this complaint, Confucius said, "Asking questions about it is indeed part of Li."

16 Confucius said, "An archery match is not about piercing through the leather of the target—but rather hitting the bull's-eye—because of the difference in the strength of the competitors. This has been the rule for ages."

16a An archery match was a ceremony included in Zhou Li (周禮). The emphasis was on the art of archery rather than brute force.

17 Zi Gong wanted to spare a lamb as a sacrifice in an official ceremony of the celebration of a New Year by the king. Confucius spoke to him, "Ci, my good student. You want to save the life of a lamb. I prefer preserving the traditional Li."

17a Zi Gong (子貢, also known as Duan Mu Ci端木賜, born around 520 BC) was one of the top ten disciples of Confucius. He later became the prime minister of the states of Lu (魯國) and Wey (衛國).

During the Zhou Dynasty, the imperial emperor traditionally held a solemn ceremony to decree the advent of a New Year and its calendar to the public.

18 Confucius said, "Serving your king [boss] in compliance with all the requirements of Li (禮) is often misunderstood by people to be flattery."

19 Ding Gong asked, "How should a king direct his ministers and how should they serve him?" Confucius replied, "A king should treat his ministers with respect and courtesy according to Li. Ministers should serve their king with loyalty."

19a Ding Gong (定公, 556–495 BC) was the duke of Lu (魯國). Confucius served him as the chief of security and justice for a few years.

20 Confucius said, "'Guan Ju' is romantic but not obscene, melancholic but not painfully sad."

20a "Guan Ju (關雎)" is the first poem in *The Book of Poetry* and a national folk song of Zhou Dynasty. It described the passion of a young man wooing a pretty girl he fantasized about (see endnote 11).

21 Ai Gong asked Zai Wo about how to make a tablet of the god of the land. Zai Wo replied, "The Xia Dynasty used pine wood. The Shang Dynasty used cypress wood. The Zhou Dynasty now uses chestnut wood. Since the word chestnut [栗] rhymes with tremble [慄], it symbolizes that people should tremble before the emperor." Confucius heard about this conversation and was disappointed but still said, "Whatever has been done does not need to be spoken of, whatever is committed and ongoing does not need to be objected, whatever is past does not need to be blamed."

21a Ai Gong (哀公) was the duke of Lu (魯國) from 494 to 468 BC.

Zai Wo (宰我, also known as Zai Yu, 宰予, 522–458 BC) was among the top disciples of Confucius and was a minister of Ai Gong. Zai Wo made a mistake by saying that people should tremble before the emperor. However, Confucius excused him for making such a mistake.

22 Confucius criticized Guan Zhong and said, "Guan Zhong was a shallow person." Somebody then asked, "Was he a modest person?" Confucius replied, "He had three secret vaults to store his personal treasures. He hired many household servants, each responsible for just a single task. How could he be modest?" Somebody then asked, "Did he follow Li?" Confucius said, "His king built a tall hedge inside the entrance to his palace. Guan Zhong did the same to his residence. His king arranged empty glasses for toasting with foreign dignities. Guan Zhong did the same. If he knew Li, who does not know Li then?"

22a Guan Zhong (管仲, 725–645 BC) was a prominent politician, philosopher, and pioneer of the School of Law (Legalism) before Confucius and was a dominant minister of the state of Qi (齊國). He helped the state of Qi become a hegemon. He advocated the implementation of tough laws and promotion of commerce for the country. Confucius did not endorse this school of thought. Instead of implementation of tough laws, Confucius supported Zhou Li as a means of ruling a country. Therefore, Confucius criticized Guan Zhong.

23 Confucius praised the music of a virtuoso from the state of Lu and said, "His music can be analyzed as follows: it begins with a lively and ebullient opening movement, followed by a reverberation of purity and elegance, and ends with a finale."

24 The governor of County Yi wanted to see Confucius who said, "I always welcome the visit of a Jun Zi." After his visit, the

governor exclaimed, "Why do you, students of the great teacher, need to worry about not finding official appointments? The entire country has been decadent for a long time. Your teacher is a siren sent by heaven."

24a Yi was a small county in the state of Lu (魯國).

25 Confucius commented on the Songs in Praise of Yao and Shun: "They are ultimately beautiful and virtuous." However, his comment on the Songs in Praise of King Wu was: "They are ultimately beautiful but not virtuous enough."

25a Yao (堯, 2356–2255 BC) and Shun (舜, 2294–2184 BC) were the two saintly kings in ancient times. King Wu of the Zhou Dynasty (周武王, died 1043 BC) was not as virtuous as them.

26 Confucius said, "Those at the top are not kind and generous; do not respect Li and mourn during their parents' funeral. How can I revere them?"

26a Confucius criticized the ruling class of his era.

CHAPTER 4

MINGLE WITH
REN (里仁)

1 Confucius said, "It is advisable to mingle with people of Ren virtue. If you choose to mix with people void of Ren, are you prudent?"

1a Ren (仁) is the collection of human virtues, including love.

2 Confucius said, "A person void of Ren virtue cannot be content to stay poor for long and cannot be happy with his affluence for long too. A person with Ren virtue is comfortable with his Ren way. A wise person knows that the Ren way is beneficial to him."

3 Confucius said, "Only those people with Ren virtue can love others and also despise some others."

4 Confucius said, "If a person is committed to practice the Ren way, he will not do evil."

5 Confucius said, "Everyone loves great wealth and high-class status. If these are obtained in improper ways, we should not pursue them. Everyone hates poverty and low-class status. If the departure

from them is through improper ways, we should not follow them. If a Jun Zi does not practice the Ren way, he does not deserve to be called a Jun Zi. A Jun Zi does not forget about the Ren way between any two meals. He sticks to it during an emergency and a crisis. He also sticks to it during hardship and distress."

5a A Jun Zi (君子) is used in Chinese scholarly texts to mean a gentleman, a person of noble character, a prominent and respectable person in society, or a person who upholds virtuous principles.

6 Confucius said, "I have not met a person who is really dedicated to the practice of Ren, and a person who detests others for lack of Ren. Those who are dedicated to Ren are unsurpassable. The latter type just tries to avoid being influenced and hurt by other lowly people. Can you devote all your energy in practicing Ren daily? I have not seen anyone who is short of ability and means to do so. There might be some, but I have not seen them yet."

7 Confucius said, "All misbehaviors and mistakes of people can be classified into categories. By noting what type of mistake a person commits, we can tell whether he has Ren virtue."

7a This sentence can also be interpreted as: "All past actions taken by people can be classified into categories. By noting what type of past actions taken by a person, we can tell whether he has Ren virtue."

8 Confucius said, "If one is enlightened with True Way in the morning, one is willing to die in the evening."

8a This sentence means that being enlightened with True Way is all that matters in life.

9 Confucius said, "Those people who claim to be practitioners of the Ren way and who hate being poor do not deserve to talk about Ren."

10 Confucius said, "In handling worldly matters, a Jun Zi does not have preconceived do's and don'ts. All acts should be guided by righteous principles."

11 Confucius said, "A Jun Zi cares about virtuous and righteous principles, whereas a Xiao Ren cares about worldly matters. A Jun Zi cares about rules and discipline, whereas a Xiao Ren cares about benefits."

11a A Jun Zi (君子) is a gentleman, a person of noble character, a prominent and respectable person in society, or a person who upholds virtuous principles. A Xiao Ren (小人) is the opposite of a Jun Zi.

12 Confucius said, "If your self-interest and advantage are the basis of your actions, you will draw antagonism."

13 Confucius said, "If you can rule a country with the principle of comity, what else is more difficult? If you cannot rule a country with the principle of comity, how would you practice Li?"

14 Confucius said, "You should not worry about not getting an official appointment. You should instead worry about whether you have the capability to take that assignment. You should not worry that people do not know you. You should instead strive for remarkable achievement."

15 Confucius said, "Shen, there is an integrating theme of my teaching." Zeng Zi replied, "Yes, sir." After Confucius left the class, other disciples asked Zeng Zi, "What does that mean?" Zeng Shen

said, "Our teacher's philosophy can be summarized by loyalty and forgiveness."

15a Zheng Zi (曾子, 505–432 BC, also known as Zheng Shen 曾參) was a top disciple of Confucius and a predominant figure in Confucianism. He authored *The Book of Great Learning* (大學) and *The Book of Filial Piety* (孝經) (see endnote 12 and reference 9).

16 Confucius said, "A Jun Zi is mindful of righteousness, whereas a Xiao Ren is mindful of self-interest and benefits."

17 Confucius said, "When you meet a virtuous person, you should strive to emulate his virtues. When you meet a person void of virtue, you should consider whether you have the same flaws."

18 Confucius said, "When your parents are wrong, you should advise them tactfully. If they do not take your advice, you should not irritate them. You cater to their needs without complaint."

19 Confucius said, "If your elderly parents are still alive, you try to avoid traveling afar. If a travel is unavoidable, you go to a designated place only."

20 Confucius said, "After your parents have died, if you follow their teaching for a long time, you are indeed a filial and pious person."

21 Confucius said, "You should know the ages of your parents. On one hand, you should be glad that they have lived to those ages. On the other hand, you should also worry that they will die soon."

22 Confucius said, "A Jun Zi in the old days did not talk indiscreetly. He would feel ashamed if he could not keep his words."

22a Jun Zi (君子) is used in Chinese scholarly texts to mean a gentleman, a person of noble character, a prominent and respectable person in society, or a person who upholds virtuous principles.

23 Confucius said, "If you practice self-control according to the rules of Li, you will make fewer mistakes."

24 Confucius said, "A Jun Zi is cautious with his words but proactive with his deeds."

25 Confucius said, "A virtuous person is never lonely because there is always a comrade nearby."

26 Zi You said, "If you nag your king [boss], you will certainly be humiliated. If you nag your friends, you will certainly be alienated."

26a Zi You (子游, also known as Yan Yan言偃, 506–443 BC) was a prominent disciple of Confucius.

CHAPTER 5

GONG YE CHANG (公冶長)

1 Confucius said of Gong Ye Chang, "He is qualified to marry my daughter although he is imprisoned not because of his own fault." Confucius's daughter then married him.

1a Gong Ye Chang (公冶長, 519–470 BC) was a disciple and a son-in-law of Confucius. The criteria under which Confucius chose a son-in-law was the person's good character rather than his wealth, status, or power.

2 Confucius said of Nan Rong, "When the country is peaceful, he managed to keep his official position. When the country is savage, he could avoid prosecution and disgrace." Confucius then endorsed the marriage of his niece and Nan Rong.

2a Nan Rong (南容) was a disciple of Confucius.

3 Confucius commented on Fu Zi Jian, "He is indeed a Jun Zi. If the state of Lu does not have Jun Zis, where did he learn his virtue?"

3a Fu Zi Jian (宓子賤 520–445 BC) was a disciple of Confucius and a prime minister of a small state.

4 Zi Gong asked Confucius, "How about me?" Confucius replied, "You are a useful utensil." Zi Gong then asked, "What type?" Confucius replied, "A holy vessel used for offering in the imperial temple."

4a Zi Gong (子貢, also known as Duan Mu Ci端木賜, born around 520 BC) was one of the top ten disciples of Confucius. He later became the prime minister of the states of Lu (魯國) and Wey (衛國). He also made a fortune in business and was the wealthiest disciple of Confucius. He advocated making money through propriety, honesty, and trust. His eloquence was also well known. After Confucius's death, Zi Gong observed six years of mourning vigil to show his deep respect for Confucius.

"A holy vessel used for offering in the imperial temple" is an analogy of a highly prestigious and predominant official in a big country.

5 Somebody commented, "Ran Yong has Ren virtue but is not eloquent enough." Confucius responded, "Why is eloquence important? A person who can defeat others with suave arguments tends to annoy and alienate people. This type of person does not know Ren. Therefore, why is eloquence needed?"

5a Ran Yong (冉雍, born 522 BC) was a top ten disciple of Confucius and later became the butler of the powerful Ji (季) family of the state of Lu (魯國).

Ren (仁) embodies all virtues of humanity, including love.

6 Confucius recommended Qi Diao Kai to take a government job. Qi declined, saying, "I am not sure I am competent enough." Upon hearing this, Confucius was pleased.

6a Qi Diao Kai (漆雕開, 540–489 BC) was a major disciple of Confucius. He declined to take a government office and instead started his own school. His teachings later became one of the eight prominent branches of Confucianism.

7 Confucius said, "If my teachings are not applicable to this world, I would rather sail a raft into the ocean. My student, You, may be the only one who dares to follow me." Zi Lu was glad to hear this comment. Confucius then said, "It is admirable that you have more courage than me. However, just brute courage is not enough."

7a The first word, "You," was the nickname of Confucius's disciple, Zi Lu (子路, 542–480 BC), who was also called Zhong You (仲由). Among Confucius's disciples, he was best known for his ability and success in statesmanship. He was noted for his valor and sense of justice, but Confucius often warned him against acting without a second thought.

8 Meng Wu Bo asked whether Zi Lu has Ren virtue. Confucius answered, "I don't know." Meng asked further. Confucius said, "Zhong You can govern a large state that has one thousand chariots, but I do not know whether he has Ren virtue." "How about Ran Qiu?" Confucius answered, "Qiu can be a governor of a province consisting of a thousand households and a hundred chariots, but I do not know whether he has Ren virtue." "How about Gong Xi Chi?" Confucius replied, "Chi can be a diplomat to receive foreign dignities in court, but I do not know whether he has Ren virtue."

8a Meng Wu Bo (孟武伯, the son of Meng Yi Zi孟懿子, ancestor of Mencius) was a minister of the state of Lu (魯國).

Zi Lu (子路, 542–480 BC also known as Zhong You 仲由) was best known for his ability and success in statesmanship. He was noted for his valor and sense of justice.

Zi You (子有, also known as Ran You, 冉有, Ran Qiu, 冉求 born in 522 BC) was the chief of staff of the Ji Si (季氏) family and a disciple of Confucius.

Gong Xi Chi (公西赤, born 509 BC) was a disciple of Confucius and was known for his eloquence and diplomatic talents.

9 Confucius asked Zi Gong, "How would you compare yourself with Yan Hui?" Gong replied, "I dare not! Hui can deduce ten truths after hearing one. I can deduce only two truths after hearing one." Confucius said, "I agree. You are indeed not as good as him."

9a Yan Hui (颜回, 521–481 BC) was the best disciple of Confucius. Confucius held him in the highest regard among his disciples.

10 Zai Yu fell asleep during the day. Confucius commented, "A rotten piece of wood cannot be carved. A wall made of dung and dirt cannot be painted. I have given up reprimanding him." Confucius then said, "My approach to dealing with people in the past was that I trusted their actions according to their words. Having learned from the behavior of Zai Yu, I have changed my approach. I listen to other people's words and then watch their actions."

10a Zai Wo (宰我, also known as Zai Yu, 宰予, 522–458 BC) was among the top disciples of Confucius and was a minister of Ai Gong (哀公).

The last sentence was a famous and salient piece of advice from Confucius: Do not readily trust other people's words. Their actions rather are more important than their words in knowing their true character.

11 Confucius said, "I have not yet met a person with staunch will." Someone then asked, "How about Shen Cheng?" Confucius replied, "He has too many vain desires and passions. How can he have a staunch will?"

11a Shen Cheng (申棖) was a disciple of Confucius. The lesson here is that a person with vain desires, ambition, and passions cannot resist temptations. By "staunch will," Confucius meant "moral strength."

12 Zi Gong said, "I hope other people will not impose on me against my will. Likewise, I will not impose on other people against their will too." Confucius said, "Ci, you may not be able to do so all the time."

12a Zi Gong (子貢, also known as Duan Mu Ci端木賜, born around 520 BC) was one of the top ten disciples of Confucius. He later became the prime minister of the states of Lu (魯國) and Wey (衛國). He also made a fortune in business and was the wealthiest disciple of Confucius. He advocated making money through propriety, honesty, and trust. His eloquence was also well known. After Confucius's death, Zi Gong observed six years of mourning vigil to show his deep respect for Confucius.

This dialogue spelled out a principle of Ren virtue. Not imposing upon other people against their will is an ideal that must also be carried out pragmatically.

13 Zi Gong said, "Our teacher's teaching on the classics can be learned by listening to him. However, his spiritual philosophy on humanity and heavenly truth cannot be learned by just listening."

13a Spiritual development cannot be learned by just reading and listening. It must be developed by meditation, enlightenment, self-refinement, practice, experience, and so on.

14 If Zi Lu is unable to put into practice a principle he has just learned, he dreads hearing another new principle.

14a Zi Lu (子路, 542–480 BC), also called Zhong You (仲由), was a disciple of Confucius and was best known for his ability and success in statesmanship. He was also noted for his valor and sense of justice.

15 Zi Gong asked, "Why was Kong Wen Zi given a posthumous name of 'Wen Zi'?" Confucius said, "He was prompt to learn. He did not feel ashamed to learn from his subordinates and people inferior to him. Hence his was revered to be a 'great scholar.'"

15a Kong Wen Zi (孔文子) was a prime minister of the state of Wey (衛國). "Wen Zi" meant a great scholar.

16 Confucius praised Zi Chan for being a Jun Zi in four ways: "He was serious and earnest in his behaviors; he was devoted to his job; he treated his people with benevolence; he governed them with righteousness."

16a Zi Chan (子產, died 552 BC, also known as Gong Sun Qiao, 公孫僑) was a prominent statesman and reputed prime minister of the state of Zheng (鄭國).

17 Confucius said, "Yan Ping Zhong was adept in building friendship with people. Therefore, people respected him during a lasting friendship."

17a Yan Ping Zhong (晏平仲, also known as Yan Yin晏嬰, 578–500 BC) was a reputed statesman and minister of the state of Qi (齊國).

18 Confucius said, "Zang Wen Zhong kept a big tortoise in his own temple whose pillars were painted with imperial patterns. He had no wisdom to do so!"

18a Zang Wen Zhong (臧文仲, died 617 BC) was a statesman of the state of Qi (齊國) before Confucius.

In the era of Spring-Autumn Period, the tortoise shell was used as a tool for oracles. According to Zhou Li (周禮), only the imperial emperor was entitled to keep a big tortoise in his temple and to decorate it with imperial patterns on the walls and pillars. Confucius therefore criticized Zang for violating the Zhou Li.

19 Zi Zhang asked Confucius, "Although Zi Wen was appointed three times the prime minister of the state of Chu, he did not show any gratification. Although he was fired three times, he did not show any grudge. He always handed over details of his policy to his successor. How was he?" Confucius replied, "He was loyal." Zi Zhang then asked, "Did he have Ren virtue?" Confucius answered, "I don't know. It is not yet Ren virtue."

Zi Zhang then asked, "Cui Zhu assassinated his boss, the duke of Qi (齊國). His colleague, Chen Wen Zi, escaped in defiance on a chariot with forty horses. After Chen arrived in another country, he lamented that it was as treacherous as the state of Qi (齊國) under Cui Zhu. Chen then left for another country. He still lamented that the next country was as treacherous as the state of Qi under Cui Zhu. He left again. Was Chen respectable?" Confucius said, "He was impeccable only." Zi Zhang then asked, "Did he have the Ren virtue?" Confucius replied, "I don't know. It is not yet Ren virtue."

19a Zi Zhang (子張, 503–447 BC) was a disciple of Confucius. Zi Wen (門子文) was once the prime minister of the state of Chu (楚國).

Cui Zhu (崔杼) was once a minister of the state of Qi (齊國).

Chen Wen Zi (陳文子) was also another minister of Qi at the same time. The theme of this paragraph is the essence of Ren virtue. Just loyalty and being impeccable are not enough.

20 Ji Wen Zi pondered three times [a long while] before he took any action. Confucius said, "Pondering twice is already sufficient."

20a Ji Wen Zi (季文子, 651–568 BC) was a nobleman and statesman of the state of Lu (魯國) before Confucius. In ancient texts, "three times" meant many times.

21 Confucius said, "My kudos to Lin Wu Zi. When his country was properly run, he appeared to be clever and wise. When his country was rotten, he pretended to be dumb. It is easy to imitate his cleverness but difficult to imitate his dumbness."

21a Lin Wu Zi (寧武子, also known as Lin Yu, 寧俞) was a statesman of the state of Wey (衛國) before Confucius.

22 When Confucius traveled to the state of Chen, he exclaimed, "Let us go home! Let us go home! I am extremely disappointed that my countrymen who have become their officials have so much hubris. They write impressive and flowery essays, but I do not know how to educate them."

22a Confucius once toured around many countries trying to preach his doctrines to rulers. He was stuck in the state of Chen (陳國) during that tour.

23 Confucius said, "Since Bo Yi and Shu Qi did not remember past grudges, they drew less resentment and antagonism."

23a Bo Yi (伯夷) and Shu Qi (叔齊) were two princes of the last duke of the feudal state of Gu Zhu (孤竹國), during the Shang Dynasty (商朝, 1766–1046 BC). Bo Yi was the eldest brother, and Shu Qi was the youngest. Before their father died, Shu Qi was nominated to be his successor. Shu Qi abdicated his throne to his eldest brother, Bo Yi, and stressed that the eldest son should be the successor to the throne according to tradition. Bo Yi refused to accept because of the respect of his father's wish. Both eventually renounced the throne and migrated to the territory of the state of Zhou (周). Later, King Wu of Zhou (周武王) raised an army to invade the Shang Dynasty. Both Bo Yi and Shu Qi knelt in front of King Wu's chariot and begged King Wu not to invade the Shang Dynasty. King Wu eventually conquered the Shang Dynasty and founded the Zhou Dynasty (周朝). Bo Yi and Shu Qi refused to be subjects of the Zhou Dynasty and eat its food. They moved to the mountains and starved to death. These two ancient characters were regarded by historians to be model Jun Zis who had the Ren virtue.

24 Confucius said, "Was Wei Sheng Gao really honest and straightforward? Somebody once asked him for a cup of vinegar. He did not reply that he did not have it. Instead, he borrowed the vinegar from his neighbor and then forwarded it to the original requestor."

24a Wei Sheng Gao (微生高) was a statesman of the state of Lu (魯國) before Confucius. He had the reputation of being straightforward. By citing this example, Confucius explained that Wei's behavior did not meet the standard of honesty. If he did not have the vinegar, he should have immediately told the requestor that he did not have it. A yes should be a yes, and a no should be a no. Do not beat around the bush.

25 Confucius said, "Flowery words, fawning smiles, and excessive courtesy are loathed by Zuo Yao Ming and me. Hiding grudges with an amicable appearance to befriend people is loathed by him and me."

25a Zuo Yao Ming (左丘明, 502–422 BC) was a reputed historian and a contemporary of Confucius, and the author of *Zuo Zhuan* (左傳), an important annotation of the *Spring-Autumn Annals* (春秋), which recorded the history of the Spring-Autumn Period (see endnote 13).

26 Yan Yuan and Zi Lu waited by the side of Confucius, who then said, "Let us talk about our wishes in life." Zi Lu said, "I wish I would share my chariots and fur coats with my friends even if they could damage them." Yan Yuan said, "I wish I would not brag about my excellence and show my achievements." Confucius said, "I wish that I can help the elderly live in comfort, I am trusted by friends, and young ones are taken care of by me with love."

26a Yan Yuan (顏淵, also known as Yan Hiu 颜回, 521–481 BC) was the best disciple of Confucius.

Zi Lu (子路, 542–480 BC), also called Zhong You (仲由), was a disciple of Confucius and was best known for his ability and success in statesmanship. He was also noted for his valor and sense of justice.

27 Confucius said, "Let us not dwell on it anymore. I have not seen anyone who, recognizing his mistakes, would sincerely repent in his heart."

28 Confucius said, "In any neighborhood of ten households, there must be someone as loyal and honest as I am. However, he may not be as earnest in the pursuit of knowledge."

CHAPTER 6

YONG YE (雍也)

1 Confucius said, "My comment on Ran Yong is that he has the caliber of being a government official."

1a Ran Yong (冉雍, born 522 BC, also known as仲弓 Zhong Gong) was a prominent disciple of Confucius.

2 Zhong Gong asked about Zi Sang Bo Zi. Confucius replied, "He is all right. Simplicity is his strength." Zhong Gong then said, "If a person takes matters seriously in his heart but practice simplicity, would he be a good ruler? On the other hand, if a person brushes over matters in his heart and practices simplicity, would he be too simple?" Confucius replied, "You are right."

2a Zi Sang Bo Zi (子桑伯子) was a person. Little was known about him.

3 Ai Gong asked Confucius, "Among your students, who is a great scholar?" Confucius said, "Yan Hui was the best. He never blamed others. He never committed the same mistake twice. Unfortunately, he died young. After his death, I have not met another great scholar."

3a Yan Hui (颜回, also known as Yan Yuan顔淵, 521–481 BC) was the best disciple of Confucius. Confucius held him in the highest regard among his disciples.

4 Zi Hua was sent as an envoy to the state of Qi. Zi You asked Confucius to give Zi Hua's mother some grains. Confucius said, "Give her 6.4 bushels." Zi You then asked for more. Confucius said, "Give her another 2.4 bushels then." Zi You secretly gave her eighty bushels instead. Confucius said, "I heard that Zi Hua traveled to the state of Qi on a chariot carried by fat horses, wearing a light warm fur coat. A Jun Zi should help the poor and needy rather than enriching the wealthy."

4a Zi Hua (子華, also known as Gong Xi Chi公西赤) was a disciple of Confucius.

Zi You (子有, also known as Ran You, 冉有, Ran Qiu, 冉求born in 522 BC) was a prominent disciple of Confucius.

5 Yuan Si was hired as the butler of Confucius's family. Confucius gave him an annual salary of nine hundred bushels of grain. Yuan Si declined such large offer. Confucius said, "Don't decline my offer. Give some to your neighbors, villagers, and clan."

5a Yuan Si (原思, also known as Yuan Xian 原憲 and Zi Si子思, born 515 BC) was a disciple of Confucius.

6 Confucius spoke of Zhong Gong to his other disciples and said, "That calf of a farm cow has red hair and straight horns. People do not use it as a sacrifice to gods because of its breed. However, do gods of mountains and rivers care about its heritage?"

6a Ran Yong (冉雍, born 522 BC, also known as仲弓 Zhong Gong) was a prominent disciple of Confucius. This paragraph has a story behind it. Ran Yong was born of a poor family. His father could not afford to send Yong to school, and the promise of sending Yong to school was delayed year after year. To support the family, his father committed theft, was imprisoned, and died in prison. The orphan Yong appeared at the doorstep of Confucius's school and begged for admission. Confucius took Yong as his student with free tuition as well as living stipends. Confucius's other disciples discriminated against Yong because of his background as the son of a criminal. Confucius loved this brilliant young Yong, foresaw that Yong would become a great man, and was determined to teach other students a lesson. During an outing in the countryside, Confucius and all his students saw an unusually beautiful young calf of a farm cow. It had red hair and straight horns. Confucius then told his students that this calf was not suitable to be a sacrifice to gods. (Note: It was a tradition that farm cows were not supposed to be used as sacrifices to gods because the breed of farm cows was not noble enough). His students disagreed and said, "Why not? Why should gods care about the heritage of this beautiful calf?" Confucius then said, "Excuse me, you guys are correct. If this logic applies to cows, would it also apply to a person?" Confucius's other disciples immediately realized their past mistake in discriminating against Yong because of his background and heritage. This paragraph gave rise to a popular Chinese proverb: "Don't disparage the calf of a farm cow."

7 Confucius said, "Yan Hui's mind does not deviate from Ren virtue for a long time, whereas other students can maintain such virtues for days only."

7a Yan Hui (颜回, also known as Yan Yuan顔淵, 521–481 BC) was the best disciple of Confucius. Confucius held him in the highest regard among his disciples.

8 Ji Kang Zi asked Confucius, "Can Zhong You be a good government official?" Confucius replied, "Zhong You is decisive. Why not?" Ji Kang Zi then asked, "Can Ci [Zi Gong] be a good government official?" Confucius replied, "Ci has great perspective. Why not?" Ji Kang Zi further asked, "How about Ran Qiu [Zi You]?" Confucius replied, "Qiu is very dexterous. Why not?"

8a Ji Kang Zi was the prime minister of the state of Lu (魯國). Confucius returned to his motherland after eight years of diplomatic tours of many countries. Ji Kang Zi sought Confucius's opinions on his disciples.

Zi Lu (子路, 542–480 BC, also known as Zhong You 仲由) was a disciple of Confucius and was best known for his ability and success in statesmanship.

Zi Gong (子貢, also known as Duan Mu Ci 端木賜, born around 520 BC) was one of the top ten disciples of Confucius.

Zi You (子有, also known as Ran You, 冉有, Ran Qiu, 冉求 born in 522 BC) was the chief of staff of the Ji Si (季氏) family and a disciple of Confucius.

Note: This paragraph described the key qualities of a good government official: decisiveness, perspective, and competency.

9 Ji Kang Zi wanted to appoint Min Zi Qian to be the governor of the province of Fei (費). Min told the messenger, "Please convey my decline of this offer. If you come back again, I will hide in the shore of River Min [which is far away]."

9a Min Zi Qian (閔子騫, 536–487 BC) was a disciple of Confucius and named as one of the twenty-four models of filial piety in the classic *The Book of Filial Piety* (孝經). He was born of a poor family. His own mother died early. His stepmother abused him and gave him a light coat in a freezing winter, whereas his two younger stepbrothers had warm and heavy coats. His father was upset when he discovered this fact and wanted to punish the stepmother by divorcing her. (In the old days, divorcing a wife meant throwing her out of the house). Instead of cheering his father's decision, Min Zi Qian begged his father to stay with the stepmother, arguing that, with the presence of the stepmother, only one boy would suffer in the cold weather, whereas in the absence of the stepmother, all three boys would suffer. His father then changed his mind. His stepmother realized her past misbehavior and repented (see reference 9).

Ji Kang Zi was a powerful but malicious and unpopular prime minister of the state of Lu (鲁國). He wanted to appoint Min Zi Qian to be the governor of a province that was granted to Ji. The young Min resented Ji's policy and declined the big offer. However, at the request of Confucius, Min eventually took the offer and ran the city well after a few years. Min then immediately quit after his mission was accomplished.

10 Bo Niu was terminally sick. Confucius visited him and held Niu's hand from outside the window. Confucius exclaimed, "We will miss a good person. It is fate! Why would a good person get such a disease? Why would a good person get such a disease?"

10a Bo Niu (伯牛) was a disciple as well as a close friend of Confucius and accompanied Confucius during Confucius's diplomatic tour of many countries. Bo Niu got a contagious disease that was incurable.

11 Confucius said, "Yan Hui is indeed virtuous. He eats with a bowl made of bamboo, drinks with a cup made of the skin of a melon, and lives in a ghetto. Other people cannot withstand such austerity. He, on the contrary, enjoys it. Yan Hui is indeed virtuous."

11a Yan Hui (颜回, also known as Yan Yuan顏淵, 521–481 BC) was the best disciple of Confucius. Confucius held him in the highest regard among his disciples.

12 Ran Qiu confessed to Confucius, "It is not because I do not like your teachings. It is because I do not have the (moral) strength to follow them." Confucius replied, "Weak persons tend to give up all their accumulated progress before the finish line. You have now returned to square one!"

12a Zi You (子有, also known as Ran You, 冉有, Ran Qiu, 冉求born in 522 BC) was the chief of staff of the Ji Si (季氏) family and a disciple of Confucius.

13 Confucius told Zi Xia, "You should be a scholar who emulates a Jun Zi rather than a Xiao Ren."

13a Zi Xia (子夏, born 507 BC) was a disciple of Confucius and later became an official of the state of Wei (魏國).

A Jun Zi (君子) is a gentleman, a person of noble character, a prominent and respectable person in society, or a person who upholds virtuous principles. A Xiao Ren (小人) is the opposite.

Confucius reminded Zi Xia before his appointment as a senior government official. A learned and intelligent scholar can become a great person if he follows the principles of a Jun Zi. On the contrary, the more knowledge he has, the more horrible he will be if he follows the Xiao Ren (小人) ways.

14 Zi You became the mayor of Wu. Confucius asked him, "Have you hired any good staff yet?" Zi You replied, "I have met a person called Dan Tai Mie Ming. He always follows the proper

channel in doing things. He never visited my house for unofficial matters," [meaning that he never seeks personal favors and fawns].

14a Zi You (子游, also known as Yan Yan言偃, 506–443 BC) was a prominent disciple of Confucius.

Dan Tai Mie Ming (澹台滅明, born 512 BC) was a disciple of Confucius. He looked ugly. Confucius belittled him in the beginning because of his appearance. After Dan demonstrated great achievements later, Confucius confessed that he had misjudged Dan. There is a popular Chinese saying: 'You don't judge a person based on his appearance."

15 Confucius said, "Meng Zhi Fan never boasted his own merit. Once upon time, his army was defeated. He stayed as the rearguard defending the army in flight. When he arrived at the gate of his home citadel, he whipped his horse and said: 'I stayed at the rear not because I dared. It was because my horse could not run fast enough.'"

15a Meng Zhi Fan (孟之反) was an army general. Confucius cited this example to teach modesty to students.

16 Confucius said, "If one does not have the eloquence of Zhu Tuo but only has the handsomeness of Song Chao, it is difficult to establish himself in today's world."

16a Zhu Tuo (祝鮀) was a minister of the state of Wey (衛國) and was known for his eloquence.

Song Chao (宋朝) was a prince of the state of Song (宋國) and was known for his handsomeness.

17 Confucius said, "Who can get outside his house without passing through the door? Why people do not follow my way?"

18 Confucius said, "If one's internal substance surpasses his external sophistication one is unrefined and crude. If one's external sophistication surpasses his internal substance, one is a charlatan and superficial. A Jun Zi should have internal substance as well as external sophistication."

19 Confucius said, "A person's survival is based on propriety. Crooked people can survive because they are lucky."

20 Confucius said, "Learned people are inferior to those who are eager to learn. Those who are eager to learn are inferior to those who enjoy learning."

21 Confucius said, "We can talk about sophisticated theory and ideology with people with above average wisdom. We cannot talk about sophisticated theory and ideology with people with below average wisdom."

22 Fan Chi asked Confucius about wisdom. Confucius said, "If you strive to promote propriety and virtuosity among your people, and if you respect gods and spirits but stay away from them, you have wisdom." Fan Chi then asked about Ren (仁). Confucius replied, "A person who practices Ren would undertake a challenge ahead of others and stay behind others in claiming credit and awards."

22a Fan Chi (樊遲, born about 505 BC) was a prominent disciple of Confucius. The sentence, "You respect gods and spirits but stay away from them" is an important teaching of Confucius. In the old days, people used to pray to gods and spirits for their blessings. Although Confucius was not an atheist, he insisted that people should strive to solve their worldly problems with real and pragmatic human means rather than unrealistic reliance on gods. This was a reminder for rulers in the old days to be proactive and to stay away from superstition. (God does not help those who do not help themselves). This teaching is still relevant in today's world.

23 Confucius said, "A wise person loves to behave like water [being versatile and flexible], whereas a person with Ren virtue loves to behave like a mountain [being steadfast, firm, and unwavering]. A wise person takes initiatives on challenges, whereas a person with Ren stays calm. A wise person lives a happy life, whereas a person with Ren virtue lives long."

24 Confucius said, "Since the state of Qi undertook its reform, it has become as good as the state of Lu. If the state of Lu takes on better reforms, it will become a utopia, which occurred in ancient times."

24a The state of Qi (齊國) was bigger but less well run than the state of Lu (魯國).

25 Confucius said, "This wine vessel has its shape but is not a real wine vessel. Is it a wine vessel? Is it a wine vessel?"

25a This paragraph has a few interpretations. The most popular interpretation is that Confucius used the wine vessel as an analogy to criticize the current decadence of governments. In the old days, the wine vessel was a utensil used in worship. Confucius lamented that rulers performing the rituals of toasting to gods with the wine vessel were rotten. The vessel had lost its purpose since gods would not be pleased. Another interpretation is that Confucius wanted his disciples to understand the difference between form versus substance. The wine vessel looks like a vessel in form, but the substance of a wine vessel is in its function. This is an analogy for a person. A person may have the appearance of a human being, but if he is rotten, he does not deserve to be a human being.

26 Zai Wo asked, "If a person with Ren virtue is told that a virtuous person fell into a well and is trapped there, should he jump into the well too?" Confucius replied, "Why should he do so? A Jun Zi should jump into the well to save life but should avoid being trapped. A Jun Zi can be deceived but should avoid entrapment."

26a Zai Wo (宰我, also known as Zai Yu, 宰予, 522–458 BC) was among the top disciples of Confucius.

27 Confucius said, "If a Jun Zi is broadly knowledgeable of the classics and abides by the rules of Li, he will not go astray."

28 Confucius visited Nan Zi. Zi Lu was upset with Confucius. Confucius swore, "If I have done anything wrong, may I be criticized by heaven!"

28a Nan Zi (南子) was a concubine of Wey Ling Gong (衛靈公), the duke of Wey (衛國). She was known to be a sexy and lustful beauty. Confucius worked for her husband as a minister. Nan Zi summoned Confucius to her private residence to test whether she could even charm Confucius who had a reputation of being a Jun Zi. When Confucius saw her, he followed all proper etiquette in royal court and did nothing wrong. Yet his student, Zi Lu, misunderstood Confucius.

Zi Lu (子路, 542–480 BC, also known as Zhong You 仲由) was a disciple of Confucius and was best known for his ability and success in statesmanship. He was noted for his valor and sense of justice.

29 Confucius said, "The doctrine of Zhong Yong is the pinnacle of all virtuous principles. Nowadays, most people have abandoned it for a long while."

29a Zhong Yong (中庸) is the central doctrine of Confucianism. Confucius's grandson Zi Si (子思) wrote *The Book of Zhong Yong* (*The Doctrine of the Mean*). Zhong means unbiased, not in excess in one way or the other, nothing more and nothing less. Yong means ordinary, commonplace, firm, unwavering, and perpetual truth (see endnote 14 and reference 10).

30 Zi Gong asked, "If one practices charity to benefit everybody and foster welfare for all people, can he be considered to have the Ren virtue?" Confucius replied, "He is not only a person with the Ren virtue. He is already a saint! Even Yao and Shun were unable to do so. When a person with the Ren virtue sets a goal, he would also help others to set the same. When he desires success in achieving the goal, he would help others to achieve the same. He can find handy occasions and circumstances in daily life to set good examples for people. This is a way to practice the Ren virtue."

30a Zi Gong (子貢, also known as Duan Mu Ci端木賜, born around 520 BC) was one of the top ten disciples of Confucius. He later became the prime minister of the states of Lu (魯國) and Wey (衛國). He also made a fortune in business and was the wealthiest disciple of Confucius. He advocated making money through propriety, honesty, and trust. His eloquence was also well known. After Confucius's death, Zi Gong observed six years of mourning vigil to show his deep respect for Confucius.

Yao (堯, 2356–2255 BC) and Shun (舜, 2294–2184 BC) were the two saintly kings of ancient times. Later historians and Confucians thought Yao and Shun founded a utopian society in China.

CHAPTER 7

JUST NARRATE (述而)

1 Confucius said, "I just narrate the classics and do not create new ideas. I believe in and appreciate ancient culture. I secretly try to emulate the ancient sage, the Old Peng."

1a Old Peng was just a symbolic sage in ancient times. Nobody knew his identity. This paragraph shows Confucius's humility.

2 Confucius said, "Keeping silently and persistently in mind what I have learned, learning relentlessly, and teaching others tirelessly are what I strive. Have I done so?"

3 Confucius said, "I worry about whether I have not cultivated my virtue, have not taught what I have learned, have not practiced righteousness I am aware of, and have not corrected my own mistakes."

4 In his home, Confucius was relaxed and comfortable.

5 Confucius said, "I am getting senile already. I have not dreamed of the duke of Zhou for a long while."

5a The duke of Zhou (周公, died 1032 BC) was the son of the King Wen (周文王, 1152–1056 BC) and the brother of King Wu (周武王, died 1043 BC), the founding fathers of the Zhou Dynasty (周朝). The duke of Zhou was regarded as the best prime minister in ancient times. He established the Zhou Li (周禮) and set up a model government for later generations. Confucius regarded him as a saint and his model.

6 Confucius said, "Set yourself on the path to morality, be guided by virtuous principles, act according to Ren, and roam the world with your skills."

6a In Confucius's era, all scholars and elites had to learn six basic skills and subjects: Li (禮), music, archery (i.e., martial arts), horse riding, classic books, and mathematics.

7 Confucius said, "Whoever brings along ten bundles or more of dry meat as tuition, I will never reject him as my student."

7a In Confucius's era, people brought along a few bundles of dry meat as a small introductory gift. Confucius asked for a small tuition. He set a low tuition fee so that poor young students could still afford the tuition. Confucius had a total of more than three thousand students, who came from a variety of families, from nobility to dire poverty. He was a trendsetter during his time by removing class discrimination and promoting social mobility. Many graduates of his school became prominent statesmen and scholars.

8 Confucius said, "The proper way to enlighten a student is as follows. Do not give him an answer until he has made a serious effort in thinking through but is still stuck. Do not teach him further if he cannot make three salient inferences from one teaching."

8a Confucius did not endorse rote learning. The student must take his own initiatives in thinking through and making new discoveries and inferences.

9 Whenever Confucius ate with someone whose family member had died, Confucius was never full.

10 Confucius did not sing on the same day he cried.

11 Confucius spoke with Yan Yuan, "If people value us, we will do our best. If not, we hide our abilities. Only you and I will do so."

Zi Lu asked Confucius, "If you are the chief commander of all armies, what type of general would you trust?" Confucius said, "I would not hire those who can kill a tiger with their bare hands, walk across the river, and fight to death without regret. I would rather hire those who can assess risks before a crisis and apply ingenious stratagems to get victory."

11a Yan Hui (颜回, also known as Yan Yuan颜渊, 521–481 BC) was the best disciple of Confucius. Confucius held him in the highest regard among his disciples.

The second point is in line with Sun Tzu's military philosophy. Use your brain rather than your brawn. Such philosophy also applies to modern management.

Zi Lu (子路, 542–480 BC also known as Zhong You 仲由) was best known for his ability and success in statesmanship. He was noted for his valor and sense of justice.

12 Confucius said, "If it is righteous and proper to become wealthy and powerful in an opportunity, I would pursue it even if it

requires me to be a lowly bodyguard. If it is not righteous and proper, I would do something else I like."

13 Confucius took serious care in three circumstances: during a period of fasting and abstinence, during a war, and during a disease.

14 When Confucius was in the state of Qi (齊國), he heard the classical music during the ancient Shun era. He was so fascinated with the music that even meat was tasteless to him for three months. He said, "I am surprised that this music is so beautiful."

14a Shun (舜, 2294–2184 BC) was the emperor of the ancient utopian period in China.

15 Ran You asked Zi Gong, "Will our teacher work for the duke of Wey (衛君)?" Zi Gong replied, "Let me ask him." Zi Gong then went in to see Confucius and asked, "Who are Bo Yi and Shu Qi?" Confucius said, "They are two ancient saints." Zi Gong asked, "Did they regret?" Confucius said, "If one wants Ren virtue and gets it, what regret does he have?" Zi Gong then went outside and told Ran You, "Our teacher won't work for the duke of Wey [because he is not a good king]."

15a Zi You (子有, also known as Ran You, 冉有, Ran Qiu, 冉求 born in 522 BC) was the chief of staff of the Ji Si (季氏) family and a disciple of Confucius.

Zi Gong (子貢, also known as Duan Mu Ci端木賜, born around 520 BC) was one of the top ten disciples of Confucius. He later became the prime minister of the states of Lu (魯國) and Wey (衛國). He also made a fortune in business and was the wealthiest disciple of Confucius. He advocated making money through propriety, honesty, and trust. His eloquence was also well known.

After Confucius's death, Zi Gong observed six years of mourning vigil to show his deep respect for Confucius.

Bo Yi (伯夷) and Shu Qi (叔齊) were two princes of the last duke of the feudal state of Gu Zhu (孤竹國), during the Shang Dynasty (商朝, 1766–1046 BC). Bo Yi was the eldest brother and Shu Qi was the youngest. Before their father died, Shu Qi was nominated to be his successor. Shu Qi abdicated his throne to his eldest brother, Bo Yi, and stressed that the eldest son should be the successor to the throne according to tradition. Bo Yi refused to accept because of the respect of his father's wish. Both eventually renounced the throne and migrated to the territory of the state of Zhou (周). Later, King Wu of Zhou (周武王) raised an army to invade the Shang Dynasty. Both Bo Yi and Shu Qi knelt in front of King Wu's chariot and begged King Wu not to invade the Shang Dynasty. King Wu eventually conquered the Shang Dynasty and founded the Zhou Dynasty (周朝). Bo Yi and Shu Qi refused to be subjects of the Zhou Dynasty and eat its food. They moved to the mountains and starved to death. These two ancient characters were regarded by historians to be model Jun Zis who had the Ren virtue.

16 Confucius said, "Eating simple meals, drinking plain water, resting on my shoulders without a pillow are very enjoyable to me. If wealth and power are obtained by improper means, I consider them to be clouds in the sky [fleeting and transient]."

17 Confucius said, "I hope I can live a few years longer. Even if I start studying *The Book of Changes* at fifty, I will not commit any mistakes later."

18 When Confucius recited *The Book of Poetry, The Book of History,* and *Zhou Li,* he used the official and national dialect of the Zhou Dynasty [and not the local dialect of the state of Lu].

19 Duke Ye asked Zi Lu about Confucius. Zi Lu did not answer. Confucius later asked Zi Lu, "Why couldn't you say that I am the type of person who forgets about his meals while studying hard, forgets about worries while playing music, and forgets about aging and dying."

19a Duke Ye (葉公) was a minister of the state of Chu (楚國).

Zi Lu (子路, 542 to 480 BC also known as Zhong You 仲由) was best known for his ability and success in statesmanship. He was noted for his valor and sense of justice.

20 Confucius said, "I was not born with knowledge. I just like ancient culture, and I am eager to learn."

21 Confucius never talked about myths, violence, revolt, gods, or spirits.

22 Confucius said, "Whenever three persons gather together, there must be somebody [or something] you can learn from. You pick the good one and emulate him [or it]. You note their mistakes and avoid committing the same yourself."

23 Confucius said, "If I am endowed with virtues by heaven, what can Huan Tui do to me?"

23a Huan Tui (桓魋) was a powerful and notorious chief commander of the state of Song (宋國). Some scholars believed that he was the brother of Si Ma Niu (司馬牛), a disciple of Confucius. In 492 BC, Confucius passed by the state of Song. Huan Tui heard about Confucius's visit to his country and planned to assassinate Confucius. While Confucius was teaching his disciple under a tree on the principles of Li, Huan Tui's men tried to kill Confucius by cutting down the tree. Fortunately, his disciples protected him so that he could escape.

24 Confucius said, "Do you, students, think that I have anything to hide from you? I have nothing to hide. There was no action that I did not do with my students together. I am this type of person."

25 Confucius taught four major subjects to students: classic scriptures, proper behaviors, loyalty, and trust.

26 Confucius said, "We may not be able to find [become] a saint. Just being a Jun Zi is good enough." Confucius said, "We may not be able to find [become] a good person. Just trying persistently to be a good person is good enough. If a person does not have a virtue but pretends to have it, or is vacuous but pretends to be full, or is poor but pretends to be wealthy, he cannot be a persistently good person."

27 Confucius used a fishing rod rather than a net to catch fish. He only shot birds in the sky and not in nests.

27a This showed that Confucius was an environmentalist in his day.

28 Confucius said, "There are some people who do not know but pretend to know. I am not that type. You acquire knowledge by listening broadly, selecting good ideas and behaviors to follow, and by observing widely. The wisdom you have acquired by active learning is secondary to inborn intuition."

29 Confucius found it difficult to communicate with and educate people from the village of Hu Xiang. One day, a young man from that village came and was received by Confucius. The

students of Confucius were perplexed. Confucius said, "I appreciate the progress he has made rather than his regression. So, why should we be so harsh on him? He has made progress by correcting his past mistakes. His progress rather than his past is important."

29a Hu Xiang is the name of an unknown village.

30 Confucius said, "Is Ren virtue far away? If you desire to have Ren virtue, it is here right now."

31 The minister of crime of the state of Chen asked Confucius, "Did King Zhao of the state of Lu comply with Li?" Confucius replied, "Yes, he did." After Confucius left the room, the minister of Chen pulled aside Wu Ma Qi, a student of Confucius, and said, "I heard that a Jun Zi does not join any gang. I think the Jun Zi we know [Confucius] has joined the gang of Duke Zhao. He married a princess from the state of Wu, called Wu Meng Zi, whose family name is the same as his. If the duke knows Li, who does not know Li then?" Wu Ma Qi later told Confucius about the minister's comment. Confucius said, "I am lucky indeed. If I have made a mistake, other people must know about it."

31a The minister of crime of the state of Chen (陳司敗) was an unknown person in literature.

Wu Ma Qi (巫馬期) was a student of Confucius.

The imperial emperor of the Zhou Dynasty had a family name of Ji. This was a popular family name. Duke Zhao of the state of Lu (魯國) had a family name of Ji. The duke of Wu (吳國) also had a family name of Ji. Therefore, Wu Meng Zi (吳孟子), being a princess of the state of Wu, also had a family name of Ji. According to the Zhou Li (周禮), people with the same family name could not get married. Therefore, Duke Zhao (昭公) violated the Zhou Li.

32 When Confucius sang a song with another person, and it was sung well, Confucius must ask that person to repeat it, and then Confucius joined the singing.

33 Confucius said, "In terms of knowledge of the classics, I think I am as good as many other people. In terms of seriously practicing the principles of a Jun Zi, I don't think I am there yet."

34 Confucius said, "I cannot claim to be a saint or a person with Ren virtue yet. However, I can claim that I try to reach those goals relentlessly and to teach my disciples tirelessly." Gong Xi Hua said, "This is exactly what I, your student, cannot emulate."

34a Gong Xi Chi (公西赤, born 509 BC, also known as Gong Xi Hua公 西華) was a disciple of Confucius and was known for his eloquence and diplomatic talents.

35 Confucius was sick. Zi Lu prayed to gods for Confucius's recovery. Confucius asked, "Does it work?" Zi Lu said, "Yes, *The Book of Prayer* said, 'We have to pray to the gods of heaven and earth.'" Confucius said, "If so, I have already prayed a long time ago."

35a Zi Lu (子 路, 542–480 BC) was also called Zhong You (仲 由). Among Confucius's disciples, he was best known for his ability and success in statesmanship. He was noted for his valor and sense of justice, but Confucius often warned him against acting without a second thought. This dialogue illustrated Confucius's attitude that one should "respect the gods and spirits but stay away from them." Confucius did not believe that praying to gods would have any material effect on his health. If praying were effective, he would have recovered a long time ago. One is blessed by gods and spirits through good deeds during his life, not just by prayer.

36 Confucius said, "Lavishness leads to decadence; austerity leads to shabbiness. One should rather be shabby than decadent."

37 Confucius said, "The mind of a Jun Zi is unruffled like an open plain. The mind of a Xiao Ren is always full of worries, anxiety, and distress."

37a This sentence has often been quoted in Chinese literature and modern conversation.

38 Confucius was gentle and serious, assertive but not aggressive, and respectful and calm.

CHAPTER 8

TAI BO (泰伯)

1 Confucius said, "Tai Bo is a good example of meritorious principles. He abdicated the throne three times quietly. Not aware of his virtue, his people never gave him a word of praise."

1a Tai Bo (泰伯) was the eldest son of King Tai (周太王) from the kingdom of Zhou, who had two other sons, Zhong Yong (仲雍) and Ji Li (季歷). The youngest son, Ji Li, had a son, Chong (昌), who was regarded the best candidate to be the future leader of the country. Tai Bo left the country with his younger brother Zhong Yong to give way to Ji Li. Because of this, King Tai designated Ji Li to be his successor so that Chong would eventually become the king of the country. Tai Bo cut his hair and put on tattoos so that people could not recognize his identity. Later, Ji Li became King Wen of Zhou (周文王), and after his death, Chong became King Wu of Zhou (周武王), who founded the Zhou Dynasty (周朝). King Wen was regarded by Confucius and other historians as a saintly king. Tai Bo abdicated the throne three times. The first time, Tai Bo left the country quietly when he was aware that his father liked the grandson Chong very much. The second time, Tai Bo returned to attend his father's funeral. Ji Li offered him the throne, but Tai Bo still rejected the offer. The third time, when Ji Li was killed in a battle, ministers in court supported Tai Bo taking the throne. Tai Bo still abdicated the throne to Chong, knowing that Chong would become a better leader. Confucius praised Tai Bo for his concession of the throne.

2 Confucius said, "Being respectful beyond Li will result in excessive burden. Being cautious but not guided by Li will result in dread. Having valor but lacking Li will result in chaos. Being blunt and ignoring Li will sound like smearing. If a Jun Zi treats his family, relatives, and natives well, his people will emulate him and practice the Ren virtue. Therefore, if a Jun Zi takes care of his old friends and comrades, his people will not be mean and petty."

2a The word Li (禮) in Confucianism and in the Chinese language in general has many meanings. In ancient times, it referred to rites, rituals, ceremonies, protocols in courts and government, discipline, regulations, law and order, respect, courtesy, and etiquette in daily life; in modern times, it refers to respect, etiquette, courtesy, presents, and gifts. In the context of this paragraph, Li refers more to etiquette, protocols, and discipline (see endnote 7).

A Jun Zi here refers to a leader, nobleman, or respectable person in the upper echelon of society.

3 Zheng Zi was once sick. He summoned his students to come to his bedside and said, "Hold my feet. Hold my hands. *The Book of Poetry* said: 'Be extremely cautious, as if on the brink of an abyss, and as if treading on thin ice.' From now on, I know how to avoid harm. My good students."

3a Zheng Zi (曾子, also known as Zheng Shen曾参, born 505 BC) was a prominent disciple of Confucius, known for his filial piety. He was the author of *The Book of Great Learning* (大學).

4 Zheng Zi was sick, and Meng Jing Zi visited him. Zheng Zi said, "The last chirps of a dying bird sound sad. The last words of a

dying person are meritorious. There are three principles of conduct that a Jun Zi should pay special attention. If you present an amiable appearance, you can avoid rancor and alienation with people. If you show a solemn face, you can induce trust from people. If you talk logically with a soft voice, you can avoid being mean and rude. Do not be carried away with trivial chores. Let your staff take care of them."

4a Meng Jing Zi (孟敬子, the son of Meng Wu Bo 孟武伯 and an ancestor of Mencius) was a minister of the state of Lu (鲁国).

Zheng Zi (曾子, also known as Zheng Shen曾参, born 505 BC) was a prominent disciple of Confucius, known for his filial piety. He was the author of *The Book of Great Learning* (大學).

5 Zheng Zi said, "Even if you are competent, you still seek advice from people who are not. Even if you are knowledgeable, you still seek opinions from people who are less. Even if you have, you pretend that you do not. Even if you are solid and full, you pretend that you are soft and empty. You do not mind being attacked or your rights being infringed. I have met an old friend who behaved in these ways."

6 Zheng Zi said, "If a person can be entrusted to assist and bring up a juvenile orphan on the throne, can be entrusted to rule a country of hundreds of square miles, and will not surrender during a life or death crisis, is such a person a Jun Zi? Of course, he is!"

7 Zheng Zi said, "One must persevere in lofty goals, because the responsibility is big and the commitment is long. Practicing and fostering the Ren virtue is a big responsibility, isn't it? Upholding this virtue until death is a long commitment, isn't it?"

8 Confucius said, "You start with studying *The Book of Poetry*, then build a foundation with Li, and then complete your curriculum with music."

8a *The Book of Poetry* (詩經) was compiled during the Zhou Dynasty (周朝, around 1043–256 BC) as a collection of national folk songs (國風), royal paeans (大雅), royal poems (小雅), and hymns (頌). The national folk songs were a collection of folk songs of various states. Royal paeans were chanted in formal occasions by the emperor and princes. Royal poems were recited in feasts. Hymns were sung during ceremonies of sacrifice in temples (see endnote 6 and reference 5).

Li (禮) in Confucianism and in the Chinese language in general has many meanings. In ancient times, it referred to rites, rituals in ceremonies, protocols in courts and government, discipline, regulations, laws and order, respect, courtesy, and etiquette in daily life; in modern times, it refers to respect, etiquette, courtesy, presents, and gifts. Li (禮) includes a set of social norms that are motivated by the inner conscience of people and entrenched in the culture rather than externally imposed by the government through decrees and legislation. In the context of *The Analects*, this word has the former meaning (see endnote 7).

9 Confucius said, "If your people's moral standards and behaviors are in line with Li and righteous principles, let them be free to do what they like. If not, you have to teach them Li and righteous principles."

9a The original Chinese text of this paragraph has three contentious interpretations due to the differences in punctuation. The first interpretation was: "You just tell your people what to do. You do not need to explain to them why." The second interpretation was: "There are two types of people: those who have high moral standards and those who do not. You let the first group do whatever they like, but you try to educate the latter group so they will adopt high moral standards." The third interpretation is shown in the above translations. The difference in interpretations is critically important to understanding Confucius's political philosophy. The first interpretation implies that Confucius advocated authoritarianism and the lack of transparency of the government. This is a grave distortion of Confucianism. The second interpretation implies that Confucius advocated discrimination and segregation of people into upper and lower classes. This also contradicts Confucius's ideal of Ren. Therefore, the third interpretation is adopted here.

10 Confucius said, "Those who crave bravery but dread poverty will tend to rebel. Those who lacks the Ren virtue will also tend to rebel under a huge stress and crisis."

11 Confucius said, "If a person, having the caliber and majestic appearance of the duke of Zhou, is arrogant and mean, all his other qualities can be disregarded."

11a The duke of Zhou (周公, died 1032 BC) was the son of the King Wen (周文王, 1152–1056 BC) and the brother of King Wu (周武王, died 1043 BC), the founding fathers of the Zhou Dynasty (周朝). The duke of Zhou was regarded as the best prime minister in ancient times. He established the Zhou Li (周禮) and set up a model government for later generations. Confucius regarded him as a saint and his model.

12 Confucius said, "It is rare to find a student who does not care about making money after three years of schooling."

12a In ancient times, official salaries were paid in bushels of grain. Earning bushels of grains means earning a salary. The phrase "three years" meant a long time.

13 Confucius said, "You should be firmly faithful to meritorious principles and be an earnest learner. You should uphold meritorious principles even in the face of death. Do not serve a ruined country. Do not reside in a chaotic country. If the world is governed properly, you offer your service. If not, you quit. People feel shameful to be poor and underprivileged in a well-run country. You should feel shameful if you are rich and aristocratic in a decadent and corrupt country."

14 Confucius said, "If the timing and circumstance are not right, do not launch an inappropriate policy."

14a This is a famous sentence in Chinese culture. It can be interpreted in at least two ways. The first interpretation is: "If you are not in an official position, you do not interfere with matters related to that position." The second interpretation is shown above. The first interpretation implies that you should not bother with other people's business. This means that you should mind your own business. This implies selfishness. Such an interpretation has been used by many modern scholars to attack Confucianism. However, this interpretation contradicts with core values of Confucianism, such as Ren virtue, righteous principles, and so on. Therefore, the second interpretation is more appropriate. The word-by-word translation of the first phrase in the original Chinese text is "If you are not in that position," but the word *position* was carried over from *The Book of Changes* (*The I Ching* 易經), where *position* meant "timing" and "situation." The second interpretation meant that if the timing and situation are not right, you should not launch an untimely and out-of-place policy. Unfortunately, the first interpretation has been widely misused to justify selfishness and apathy. This has affected the Chinese ethos negatively for many centuries.

15 Confucius said, "From the overture played by the grand master to the final chorus singing the 'Guan Ju,' the entire performance was so fascinating to the ear."

15a "Guan Ju (關雎)" is the first poem in *The Book of Poetry* and a national folk song of Zhou Dynasty. It described the passion of a young man wooing a pretty girl he fantasized about (see endnote 11).

16 Confucius said, "Some people are boastful, crooked, naive, and reckless. They appear trustworthy but are in fact dishonest. I do not understand why they are like that."

17 Confucius said, "The right attitude in learning is to reach for a higher inaccessible goal and to be wary of losing what has been learned."

18 Confucius said, "Their greatness was towering and tall. Emperor Shun and Emperor Yu became leaders of the world not through conquests."

18a Yao (堯, 2356–2255 BC) chose Shun (舜, 2294–2184 BC) as his successor. Shun in term chose the Great Yu of Xia Dynasty (禹, around 2237–2139 BC) as the successor. These three kings are regarded by historians as saints. Succession to the throne at that time was determined by the caliber, character, and track record of the candidate rather than by birth or force.

19 Confucius said, "Really great! Emperor Yao's greatness was towering and tall. The sky is high, and only Yao's greatness could match it. His benevolence was so broad that his people could not find a word for it. His achievements were as great as a high mountain. His writings have shone for ages."

19a Yao (堯, 2356–2255 BC) was regarded as a saintly emperor who founded a utopian society in ancient China.

20 Shun had five competent ministers, and the country was well governed. King Wu of the Zhou Dynasty said, "I have ten competent ministers." Confucius said, "It is difficult to find talents. They are good examples. During the era of Tang and Yu, there were many competent talents. There were one woman and nine men in King Wu's cabinet. Although he had already conquered two-thirds of the country, he still paid homage to the emperor of Yan. This showed the exceptional virtue of this founder of the Zhou Dynasty."

20a The earliest dynasty in China with documented history was Tang (唐) whose leader was Yao (堯, 2356–2255 BC). The next dynasty was Yu (虞朝) whose leader was Shun (舜, 2294–2184 BC). Zhou was a feudal state of the Yan (殷朝) Dynasty, which was also known as the Shang Dynasty (商朝). King Wu of Zhou (周武王, died 1043 BC) overthrew the Shang Dynasty and founded the Zhou Dynasty (周朝). Yao, Shun, and King Wu are regarded by historians as saintly kings.

21 Confucius said, "I cannot find any flaw with the Great Yu. He ate basic meals but provided elaborate offerings to gods and spirits. He put on casual attire daily but wore elegant gowns during worship. His palace was modest. He devoted his best effort in the large-scale project of curbing floods for the country. He was really impeccable."

21a Great Yu of Xia Dynasty (禹, around 2237–2139 BC) was regarded as a saintly king by historians. He was famous for his work in constructing a large-scale water-control system for the country by reshaping land contours and rerouting rivers. Floods posed a major threat to the survival of the country at the time.

CHAPTER 9

CONFUCIUS SELDOM TALKED ABOUT (子罕)

1 Confucius seldom talked about material benefits. He preferred to talk about divine providence and Ren virtue.

2 Somebody from Da Xiang Dang commented, "Is Confucius really great? He is learned but not famous in anything." After hearing this comment, Confucius spoke to his disciples jokingly, "What expertise do I need to have? Horse riding and driving chariots? Archery? Oh, I am perhaps good at horse riding and driving chariots."

2a Da Xiang Dang was the name of a small town.

3 Confucius said, "Hats made of linen used to be worn during special rituals. Nowadays, people wear hats made of raw silk because it is cheaper. In the past, when ministers entered the imperial court, they used to kowtow to the king twice, first in the lower exterior court and next in the interior court. Nowadays, they walk straight to the interior court and kowtow once to the king. This is a sign of arrogance and disrespect. I prefer the old way."

4 Confucius has four ultimate mindsets for perfection: no prejudice, no absolute must, no fixation, no self.

4a The Chinese text of these four mindsets has many deep meanings and can be translated in myriad ways. The above translation is the most popular one among modern scholars and easiest to understand for beginners. These four mindsets need further explanation as follows:

> No Prejudice: The modern but quite superficial interpretation here is that one should not draw a conclusion based on preconceived views and beliefs and ignore solid objective facts and evidence. The deeper interpretation is that all our knowledge and concepts of phenomena (appearances) of the world are based on external signals (data) received by our senses, perceived by our brains, and analyzed and processed by our brains to form cognitive knowledge based on memory and logical reasoning. Such processes may be subject to errors, bias, inaccuracy, prejudice, and preexisting stances. Therefore, whatever we think is real and correct may not be real and correct at all. (Referring to the story of four blind men touching an elephant, each man drew a different conclusion about the shape of an elephant because of the difference in stance, limitation of sensation, and perception). Therefore, we need to be humble, open-minded, and aware of our own limitations.
>
> No Absolute Must: The modern interpretation is close to random probability theory and quantum theory. This view is that we should not think that any event must be possible or impossible with

certainty, must occur in a certain predictable way, that any person is good or bad with certainty, or that a future scenario must happen. There are many unknowns in the world, and occurrences of events may be subject to chance (and hence luck). *The Book of Changes (I Ching*易經*)*, which was annotated by Confucius, has a chapter on randomness and unexpected crises. The teaching of this philosophy is that we should have reservations on our predictions, expectations, and preconceived knowledge. If a disaster occurs beyond our expectations, we should not be too unhappy or disturbed by it. If we have a great fortune, we should not be too happy about it.

No Fixation: This translation is easier to understand for beginning readers. The deeper meaning of this mindset is close to *The Book of Changes (The I Ching* 易經*)*. Everything in the world (and the universe for that matter) changes and is transient. Nothing can be held constant in perpetuity. Because of this, we should not hold onto anything (material, mental, intellectual, or spiritual) and expect it to last without change. Therefore, we should not be stubborn about upholding our attitudes, opinions, and beliefs. We need to be receptive to new facts, discoveries, ideas, suggestions, methods, and knowledge.

No Self: On a superficial level, this can be interpreted to mean that one should consider the interest of others while sacrificing his own interest. A more serious criteria under Confucianism is the readiness to sacrifice one's life to uphold the Ren virtue, to be loyal, to keep a noble promise, or and to do good to the world at large. The deeper ideal of "no self" is that one should relinquish the concept of self in one's mind (and subconscious mind). If one does not hold onto "self," one's mind will then be connected and harmonize with everything in the universe so that one's "self" is integrated with everything else as if all things are one and the same. There is no distinction between one's "self" versus others. Doing good to anybody or anything is the same as doing good to oneself. Such a mindset is the ultimate sanctification criterion.

This short sentence in the Chinese text encapsulates a vast amount of deep philosophy of Confucianism.

5 Confucius's life was at risk while he was captured in the county of Kuang. He told his disciples, "After the death of King Wen, I have inherited all documentations of the Zhou civilization here. If heaven wants to destroy such treasures, they cannot be in my possession. If heaven does not want to destroy them, what can the people of Kuang do to me?"

5a The county of Kuang (匡) was once pillaged by Yang Huo (陽貨, also known as Yang Hu 陽虎), a national of the state of Lu (魯國). It so happened that Confucius looked like Yang Huo. When Confucius visited the county, its people mistook Confucius for Yang Huo and captured Confucius and his disciples. Confucius said the above words to console his disciples. The logic of this paragraph can be explained as follows: (1) If heaven wants to destroy such treasures, they cannot be in Confucius's possession. (2) Since they are already in Confucius's possession, by contrapositive inference from point 1, heaven does not want to destroy such treasures. (3) Since heaven does not want to destroy such treasures, the people of Kuang cannot do anything to hurt Confucius.

6 A prime minister asked Zi Gong, "Is your teacher a saint? Why is he so dexterous?" Zi Gong answered, "Since he is a saint sent by heaven, he is very dexterous." Having heard such conversation, Confucius said, "Does that minister know me? Because I was born in a poor and lowly family, I had to learn to do many menial tasks. Am I good at many skills? Not at all."

6a Zi Gong (子貢, also known as Duan Mu Ci端木賜, born around 520 BC) was one of the top ten disciples of Confucius. He later became the prime minister of the states of Lu (魯國) and Wey (衛國). He also made a fortune in business and was the wealthiest disciple of Confucius. He advocated making money through propriety, honesty, and trust. His eloquence was also well known. After Confucius's death, Zi Gong observed six years of mourning vigil to show his deep respect for Confucius.

7 Lao said, "Confucius once said that because he could not get a government job when he was young, he learned many other skills."

7a Some scholars think that Lao (牢) was a disciple of Confucius, but others do not think so.

8 Confucius said, "Am I knowledgeable? Not at all. Once upon a time, a villager asked me about something I knew nothing about. I just listened carefully, asked, and discussed the question from both angles, and then I found out the answer for him."

9 Confucius said, "The phoenix has not come. The Oracle Plaque has not emerged from the Yellow River. Alas, I am waiting all my life in vain."

9a According to ancient Chinese mythology, the phoenix is a heavenly bird and its appearance is an auspicious sign for the world. An ancient Chinese legend had a story that a dragon and a horse once emerged from the Yellow River carrying a chart that had the picture of eight key patterns to all the oracles. Such oracles were further developed into sixty-four hexagrams in *The Book of Changes* (*The I Ching* 易經). The methods and oracles described in *The Book of Changes* were originally used for divination and fortune-telling. The appearance of the phoenix and the emergence of the Yellow River chart were used in classic Chinese literature to symbolize the advent of a great leader, a great saintly king, or the birth of a new utopian society (see endnote 15).

During Confucius's era, the country was corrupt, decadent, and chaotic. There were frequent wars between many feudal states. Confucius lamented that his hope of such an auspicious future had been in vain.

10 Whenever Confucius encountered funeral mourners, noblemen, or blind men on the street, he bowed to them—even if they were young. If he needed to pass them, he walked quickly in order not to block their way.

11 Yan Yuan exclaimed, "Regarding Confucius's teaching, its peak keeps rising the more you look up at it, its strength is firmer the more you drill into it, and when it appears in front of you, it suddenly appears at your back. Our teacher steadfastly and patiently enlightens people. He teaches me the classics and restraints me with Li. I cannot stop practicing his teaching. I am exhausted since the goal is too high. I try to reach it but do not know how to start."

11a Yan Hui (颜回, also known as Yan Yuan顏淵, 521–481 BC) was the best disciple of Confucius. Confucius held him in the highest regard among his disciples.

12 Confucius was terribly ill. Zi Lu sent a disciple of Confucius in disguise as his potential funeral director. Confucius recovered

later and said, "Zhong You has committed this deception for a long while. I am not entitled to have a personal funeral director but pretend to have one. Who do I want to deceive? Do I want to deceive heaven? If I were to die in the hands of a funeral director, I would rather die in the hands of my students. Although I may not have an elaborate funeral, my body would not be thrown to the roadside."

12a Zi Lu (子路, 542–480 BC) was also called Zhong You (仲由). Among Confucius's disciples, he was best known for his ability and success in statesmanship.

In Confucius's era, only high-ranking government officials and the ruling class were entitled to hire funeral directors in preparation for their death. An elaborate funeral symbolized the prominence and status of the dead person. Since Confucius had no official role, he was not entitled to hire a funeral director.

13 Zi Gong asked, "If you have a piece of precious jade, would you store it in a vault or find a good buyer and sell it at a high price?" Confucius replied, "Sell it! Sell it! I would wait for a good buyer."

13a A piece of precious jade symbolized a competent Jun Zi. The subtle meaning of this dialogue is that a capable Jun Zi should not waste his talents. When a good opportunity arises, he should offer his service to the right employer. Zi Gong asked this question because he was looking for an official appointment. He asked Confucius whether he should take an offer if one arises.

14 Confucius planned to live in a barbaric place. Somebody commented, "That place is uncivilized and backward. How can you live there?" Confucius said, "If a Jun Zi lives there, how uncivilized and backward can it be?"

15 Confucius said, "After I have returned to my motherland, the state of Lu, from the state of Wey, I had the time to compile an album of classical music and to catalog royal paeans and hymns."

15a In 484 BC, Confucius finally returned to his motherland from the state of Wey (衛國), after fourteen years of visit to many countries, trying to preach his philosophy to their rulers.

The Book of Poetry (詩經) can be divided into national folk songs (國風), royal paeans (大雅), royal poems (小雅), and hymns (頌). The national folk songs were a collection of folk songs from various states. Royal paeans were chanted in formal occasions by the emperor and princes. Royal poems were recited at feasts. Hymns were sung during ceremonies of sacrifice in temples.

16 Confucius said, "When I am away from home, I serve kings and dukes. At home, I serve my parents and elder brothers. I take the funerals of ancestors and parents seriously. I am not addicted to alcohol. These are not difficult for me at all."

17 At the riverside, Confucius said, "Time passes like water running downstream. It does not return."

18 Confucius lamented, "I have never seen anyone who loves virtues as much as sexy women."

18a This is so true in general. Confucius uttered this in an embarrassing occasion. He resigned as a minister of the state of Lu (魯國) in 495 BC after losing a political fight. He then worked for Wey Ling Gong (衛靈公), the duke of Wey (衛國), who was a lascivious person. His concubine, Nan Zi (南子), was known to be a sexy and lustful beauty. In about one month after Confucius was hired, Wey Ling Gong tested Confucius's subservience. In a public parade, Wey Ling Gong assigned Confucius to sit next to a guard in the front carriage of the procession, which was supposedly reserved for bodyguards. Such a seating assignment was a deliberate act of humiliation. Wey Ling Gong sat with his sexy concubine in a lavish carriage in the center of the procession. (Note: in those days, the official status of a concubine was lower than that of a minister). Feeling humiliated, Confucius uttered the above words. Confucius resigned from his job nine months afterward.

19 Confucius said, "Suppose that I undertake to erect a mountain, which could be completed except for the pouring of the last bucket of earth. If I give up at this stage, it is my fault to stop. Suppose that I undertake to flatten a cavity that could be filled except for the pouring of the last bucket of earth. If I finish the job, it is my determination to go ahead."

19a This paragraph sounds mundane, but it has a very deep meaning. There are two lessons here. The first is that we should persist until the very end in achieving our goals in life and accomplish them completely. The second lesson is that success or failure in any undertaking is due entirely to our determination and persistence— and to nothing else and nobody else.

The second lesson is an important doctrine of Confucianism: "We, not heaven, determine our own fates."

This paragraph led to a common Chinese saying: "The undertaking failed because the last bucket of earth is missing."

A famous ancient Chinese parable on persistence is related to this paragraph:

> Once upon a time, there was a dumb old man, called Grandpa Dummy, who was already ninety years old. He lived in a village surrounded by two

large and tall mountains. One must overcome the mountains with precipitous heights and hazardous paths to travel to the outside world. Grandpa Dummy decided one day to move the mountains. He summoned his sons and grandchildren to move the rocks and earth of the mountains bucket by bucket. A year passed by, and little was moved, but many villagers—young and old, strong and weak, widows and orphans—were impressed and joined his project. Another old man, Grandpa Wise, came along and jeered at him, saying to Grandpa Dummy, "You are already ninety years old and will soon die. How can you complete your stupid project?" Grandpa Dummy replied, "It does not matter. After I die, my sons, grandsons, and all future descendants will carry on the project. These mountains will one day be moved." God in heaven heard such dialogue, was impressed with Grandpa Dummy's determination and persistence, and sent two angels to move the mountains for the village.

20 Confucius said, "Yan Hui is the one who follows and practices relentlessly my teachings."

20a Yan Hui (颜回, also known as Yan Yuan顏淵, 521–481 BC) was the best disciple of Confucius. Confucius held him in the highest regard among his disciples.

21 Confucius said of Yan Yuan, "Impressive indeed! I always see his progress and have never noticed his pause."

21a Yan Hui (颜回, also known as Yan Yuan顏淵, 521–481 BC) was the best disciple of Confucius. Confucius held him in the highest regard among his disciples.

22 Confucius said, "Some sprouts may not produce blossoms, and some blossoms may not produce fruits."

22a In this paragraph, sprouts, blossoms, and fruits symbolize various stages of personal development in the pursuit of knowledge and virtues. Some people lack persistence and give up in the middle of their endeavors. They are like sprouts that do not yield any fruit.

23 Confucius said, "We should feel threatened by young people because they might supersede us. Those forty- and fifty-year-olds who have not made a mark in life are not a threat at all."

24 Confucius said, "Everybody would abide by the letter of the laws, but it is more important to improve one's behavior by internalizing the spirit of laws. Everybody would be happy to hear words of praise, but it is more important to critically analyze the basis of such words. I do not know how to educate those who are happy to hear words of praise but do not think critically or those who follow laws passively but make no effort to improve their behavior."

25 Confucius said, "Emphasize loyalty and trustworthiness. Do not mingle with people of lower moral standard than yours. Do not be afraid to correct your mistakes."

26 Confucius said, "The chief commander of an army can be captured, but the will of a man cannot."

27 Confucius said, "Who does not feel ashamed when he, dressed in a shabby and worn-out gown, stands next to another guy dressed in an expensive fur coat? Perhaps Zhong You is the person. *The Book of Poetry* says: 'Don't be jealous, don't envy. Is it not great?'" After hearing such praise, Zhong You recited this verse all the time. Confucius reminded him and said, "Just doing this is not good enough."

27a Zi Lu (子路, 542–480 BC, also called Zhong You 仲由) was a disciple of Confucius. Among Confucius's disciples, he was best known for his ability and success in statesmanship. He was noted for his valor and sense of justice, but Confucius often warned him against acting without a second thought.

This paragraph talks about moral strength. One should be able to walk with kings and not feel inferior or live in poverty and not feel ashamed.

28 Confucius said, "It is only during the cold winter when we notice that pine trees are the last to shred their leaves."

28 Pine trees in this paragraph symbolize a person with endurance, perseverance, and tenacity who can withstand harsh tests and still prevail. Only harsh tests can reveal a person's inner strength.

29 Confucius said, "Wise people never become disorientated and go astray; people with Ren virtue are never beset with worries; brave people are never gripped with fears."

30 Confucius said, "Among those who learn together, some may not follow the way to moral excellence. Among those who follow such a way, some may not persist. Among those who persist, some may not practice it flexibly."

31 A poem verse said, "The flowers of primrose tree flutter in the wind. How can I forget you? My home is too far away." Confucius said, "The author was not serious about 'thinking of you.' If he was indeed serious, no place was too far away."

31a The lesson of this paragraph is that if one is serious about their goals, there should be no excuse for not attaining them.

CHAPTER 10

CLAN (鄉黨)

1 When Confucius mingled with his clansmen, he was quiet and reserved as if he was dumb. However, inside the royal temple and royal court, he spoke eloquently but cautiously.

2 Before the king arrived at a royal meeting with ministers, Confucius chatted succinctly and affectionately with colleagues and junior ministers and assertively with senior ministers. After the king arrived, Confucius spoke respectfully and cautiously.

3 When the king ordered Confucius to receive a guest, Confucius immediately put on a solemn gesture and quickened his steps. When he stood by the side of the guest, Confucius bowed with both hands out. The clothes in front and at the back were properly dressed. He walked forward like the flight of a bird. After the guest left, Confucius reported to the king and said, "Our guest has left and did not look back."

3a This demonstrated the proper etiquette.

4 When Confucius passed through the door to the royal court, he walked cautiously and respectfully as if the door was narrow. He did not stand in the middle of the door and step on its threshold.

When he passed in front of the king, he acted solemnly, walked speedily, and talked with a low voice as if he were out of breath. When he walked across the hall of the royal court, he pulled up his gown respectfully and steadfastly, holding his breath. After he left the hall and descended the steps, he looked relieved and relaxed. At the end of the stairway, he walked quickly as if he had wings. After he reached his designated mat, he resumed his solemn posture.

4a That was the expected etiquette of his time. There was no chair. People sat on mats on the floor.

5 When Confucius met the monarch of another country during a diplomatic mission, he held out an oblong jade emblem that signified his rank and bowed respectfully as if he was subservient. He raised the emblem to show respect and lowered it when he listened. His face looked nervous. He steps were tight as if he walked along a track. He smiled when he presented a gift. He was relaxed during informal and private meetings with monarchs.

6 The following were some clothing guidelines for a typical nobleman and senior official. Cloth in dark green [worn during fasting period] and black should not be used to decorate the seam of a garment. Clothes in red and purple should not be worn at home and during casual occasions because these colors were intended for important official occasions. In the summer, shirts made of light or heavy linen were worn with underwear. A black gown made of lamb leather should be covered with a cape made of dark lamb fur. A white gown should be covered with a cape made of white lamb fur. A yellow gown should be covered with fox fur. Casual wear at home should be long with a shorter right sleeve. Pajamas should be worn in bed and be longer than the height of the person by half of his height. Seating cushions were made of thick fox skin. No ornaments should be worn during a funeral. Informal garments must be tailored. Capes and hats made of black lamb leather should not be worn

during funerals. An official garment must be worn during the royal court meeting occurring on the first day of every month.

7 During a fasting period, one must put on a light-colored robe made of coarse linen [and not silk], change his diet [and abstain from wine and spices], and change his bedroom and seat [in order to separate from his wife and abstain from sex].

8 When Confucius ate, he preferred finely ground grain and finely cut meat. He did not eat overcooked and charred grains, stale fish, or rotten meat. If the food was discolored or had a bad flavor, he did not eat. If the food was not cooked well, he did not eat. If the ingredients were out of season, he did not eat. If the meat was not finely cut, he did not eat. He did not eat food without the proper sauce. Even when meat was abundantly served, he ate less meat than other food items. He could drink a lot, but he never got drunk. He did not take meat and wine bought from street hawkers. He ate a small amount of ginger at every meal.

9 Confucius did not eat the sacrificial meat leftover for one more day after the worship ceremony. Since the sacrificial meat was placed on the altar for two days, the meat would be stale after three days and become unhealthy to eat.

9a After an official worship ceremony, the organizer (usually the head of state) distributed the sacrificial meat to all participants. Since the worship ceremony usually took at least two days, such meat would be spoiled and unhealthy after three days.

10 Confucius did not talk when he was eating or in bed.

11 During a minor worship ceremony in which simple coarse grain, vegetable soup, and melon were used as sacrifice, Confucius still took the ceremony seriously by fasting beforehand.

11a In ancient times, people bathed and fasted to cleanse the body and soul before attending an important worship ceremony.

12 Confucius did not sit on a cushion that was not set up properly.

12a In Confucius's era, there were no chairs. People sat on cushions placed on the ground.

13 When a banquet in the village was over, Confucius did not leave until all the elderly guests with walking sticks had exited.

14 During a ritual to expel evil spirits, Confucius put on official attire and stood on the east side of the altar.

15 After Confucius had completed his diplomatic visit to another country, he bade farewell to the host by bowing twice.

16 Ji Kang Zi gave Confucius some medicine when he was sick. Confucius thanked him but said, "Since I do not know the effect of this medicine, I dare not take it."

16a Ji Kang Zi (季康子, died 468 BC) was the prime minister of the state of Lu (魯國) during the reign of Ai Gong (哀公) and was the most powerful official.

17 The horse barn of Confucius's house was on fire. Confucius returned home after work and asked, "Was any person hurt?" He did not ask about the horses.

18 When the king gave Confucius food for dinner, he placed the dish at the center of the table and then tasted it. When the king gave Confucius fresh meat, he cooked it and shared it with others. When the king gave Confucius a live animal, he raised it. When

Confucius dined with the king, Confucius tasted the food before the king conducted a worship ritual with the food.

19 The king visited Confucius when he was on his sickbed. Confucius turned his head toward the east and put on his official garment with a loose belt.

20 When the king summoned Confucius, he did not wait for the horse carriage to be ready. Instead, he walked hurriedly to meet the king.

21 When Confucius entered the Imperial Temple, he asked about every detail of the rituals and etiquette therein.

21a The Imperial Temple housed the shrines of all the ancestors and relatives of the king's family and the important heroes of the state. It was regarded as the most sacred place in the palace and royal court. Confucius asked about every detail therein so that he would not make any disrespectful errors.

22 Confucius's friend died, and his family and relatives could not afford to pay for his funeral and tomb. Confucius said, "Let me pay for them."

23 When receiving a gift from a friend, Confucius did not bow to show his thanks even if the gift was as valuable as a carriage and a horse. Confucius bowed only if the gift was a piece of sacrificial meat.

23a In Confucius' era, people shared sacrificial meat after a worship ceremony only with close relatives and participants of the ceremony. The giving of sacrificial meat symbolized kinship and close ties. To Confucius, the meaning of the gift was more important than its material value.

24 Confucius did not lie down in bed like a corpse. At home, he was relaxed and casual.

24a Although Confucius insisted on the adherence to Li (禮), this paragraph showed that he was casual and relaxed in his private life.

25 When Confucius met a mourner in the street, he would show a solemn face even if the mourner was a close friend. When Confucius met a person in an official uniform or a blind person on the street, Confucius showed respect. When Confucius's carriage came across a funeral procession, he bowed down and rested his head on the front bar of the carriage to show respect. He did the same when his carriage came across an official librarian carrying books (on wooden boards). When he was invited to a banquet, he showed appreciation before he ate. During a big thunderstorm, Confucius appeared uneasy.

26 Confucius first stood straight and then held the grab bar to enter the carriage safely. Once inside the carriage, he did not look back, yell, or point at people.

27 Confucius took a walk in the mountain with his students and saw a flock of wild chickens. When Confucius changed his gesture slightly, the chickens spontaneously flapped their wings, flew away, and regrouped. Confucius lamented, "These mountain chickens can react in such a short time. Amazing indeed!" When Zi Lu bent down in front of the chicken, they immediately fluttered their wings three times and flew away.

CHAPTER 11

GRASSROOTS SCHOLARS (先進)

1 Confucius said, "Those who studied Li and music before becoming government officials tend to come from the grass roots. Those who studied Li and music after becoming government officials tend to come from the elite class of the society. I would rather hire the former."

2 Confucius said, "All my disciples who followed me to the states of Chen (陳) and Cai (蔡) have left my school already."

3 Among Confucius's disciples, the most distinguished for their virtues: Yan Yuan (顏淵), Min Zi Qian (閔子騫), Ran Bo Niu (冉伯牛), Zhong Gong (仲弓); for their ability in speech: Zai Wo (宰我), Zi Gong (子貢); for their administrative ability: Ran You (冉有), Ji Lu (季路); for their literary achievements: Zi You (子遊), Zi Xia (子夏).

3a Yan Hui (颜回, also known as Yan Yuan顏淵, 521–481 BC) was Confucius's best disciple. Confucius held him in the highest regard among his disciples.

Min Zi Qian (閔子騫, 536–487 BC) was a disciple of Confucius and named as one of the twenty-four models of filial piety in the classic *The Book of Filial Piety* (孝經).

Ran Bo Niu (冉伯牛 born 544 BC) was a disciple as well as a close friend of Confucius and accompanied Confucius during Confucius's diplomatic tour of many countries. He was once a minister of the state of Lu (魯國).

Ran Yong (冉雍, born 522 BC, also known as 仲弓 Zhong Gong) was a prominent disciple of Confucius.

Zai Wo (宰我, also known as Zai Yu, 宰予, 522–458 BC) was among the top disciples of Confucius.

Zi Gong (子貢, also known as Duan Mu Ci 端木賜, born around 520 BC) was one of the top ten disciples of Confucius. He later became the prime minister of the states of Lu (魯國) and Wey (衛國). He also made a fortune in business and was the wealthiest disciple of Confucius. He advocated making money through propriety, honesty, and trust. His eloquence was also well known. After Confucius's death, Zi Gong observed six years of mourning vigil to show his deep respect for Confucius.

Ran You (冉有, also known as Zi You, 子有, Ran Qiu, 冉求 born in 522 BC) was the chief of staff of the Ji Si family and a disciple of Confucius.

Zi Lu (子路, 542–480 BC was also called Zhong You, 仲由, Ji Lu, 季路). Among Confucius's disciples, he was best known for his ability and success in statesmanship. He was noted for his valor and sense of justice, but Confucius often warned him against acting without a second thought.

Zi You (子游, also known as Yan Yan言偃, 506–443 BC) was a prominent disciple of Confucius.

Zi Xia (子夏, born 507 BC) was a disciple of Confucius and later became an official of the state of Wei (魏國).

The above were the ten most distinguished disciples of Confucius.

4 Confucius said, "Yan Hui has not helped me to advance my virtue because he followed my teachings gladly [and has never questioned them]."

5 Confucius said, "Min Zi Qian is a model of filial piety. Nobody doubts the praise of him given by his father, stepmother, and stepbrother."

5a Min Zi Qian (閔子騫, 536–487 BC) was a disciple of Confucius and named as one of the twenty-four models of filial piety in the classic *The Book of Filial Piety* (孝經). He was born of a poor family. His own mother died early. His stepmother abused him and gave him a light coat in a freezing winter, whereas his two younger stepbrothers had warm and heavy coats. His father was upset when he discovered this fact and wanted to punish the stepmother by divorcing her. (In the old days, divorcing a wife meant throwing her out the house). Instead of cheering his father's decision, Min Zi Qian begged his father to stay with the stepmother, arguing that, with the presence of the stepmother, only one boy would suffer in the cold weather, whereas in the absence of the stepmother, all three boys would suffer. His father then changed his mind. His stepmother realized her past misbehavior and repented.

6 Nan Rong recited three times the verse in *The Book of Poetry* that said: "A flaw on a piece of white jade can be removed; a bad word from the mouth cannot be rescinded." Confucius was so

impressed that he agreed to the marriage between Nan Rong and the niece of Confucius.

6a Nan Rong (南容) was a disciple of Confucius.

7 Ji Kang Zi asked Confucius, "Among your disciples, who is a great scholar?" Confucius said, "Yan Hui was a great scholar, but it is a pity that he died young. I now cannot find another one like him."

7a Ji Kang Zi (季康子, died 468 BC) was the prime minister of the state of Lu (魯國) during the reign of Ai Gong (哀公) and was the most powerful official.

Yan Hui (颜回, also known as Yan Yuan顔淵, 521–481 BC) was the best disciple of Confucius. Confucius held him in the highest regard among his disciples.

8 Yan Yuan died. His father, Yan Lu, could not afford to buy an outer casket for his son and begged Confucius to sell his carriage to pay for an outer casket. Confucius said, "Yan Yuan was a great scholar, and my son, Li, was not. I consider both as my sons. When Li died, he also had an inner coffin only and no outer casket. If I buy an outer casket for him, I will need to walk to work. Since I cannot fall behind other government officials in a procession, I need a carriage."

8a Yan Hui (颜回, also known as Yan Yuan顔淵, 521–481 BC) was the best of Confucius's disciples. Confucius held him in the highest regard among his disciples.

Yan Lu (颜路) was the father of Yan Yuan and a disciple of Confucius.

Li (鯉) was Confucius's son who died at the age of fifty.

In ancient times, wealthy people and elites were buried in an inner coffin, embedded inside an expensive, elaborately decorated outer casket, which had only ornamental value. Common people could only afford an inner coffin.

This case showed Confucius's pragmatism.

9 Yan Yuan died. Confucius mourned, "Alas! God is killing me! God is killing me!"

10 Yan Yuan died. Confucius wailed in grief. His disciples consoled him, "Master, your grief hurts yourself." Confucius said, "Am I in deep grief? If I do not mourn painfully for this man, who else should I mourn?"

11 Yan Yuan died. Confucius's disciples planned an elaborate funeral for Yan Yuan. Confucius objected to an elaborate funeral. His disciples ignored his objections and buried Yan Yuan with an elaborate funeral. Confucius said, "Yan Yuan looked upon me as his father. I have not treated him like my son yet. I now do not have a chance to make a call regarding his funeral. You guys have already taken away my role as a father."

11a In the old days, an elaborate funeral was reserved for noblemen and the elite class. It was against Li (禮) for common people to be treated with an elaborate funeral. Therefore, Confucius objected to an elaborate funeral for Yan Yuan.

12 Ji Lu asked about how to serve and worship gods and spirits. Confucius said, "You still have not served men well. Why do you bother serving gods and spirits?" Li Lu then ventured to ask about death and the afterlife. Confucius said, "You don't even know enough about life, why do you bother to know about death?"

12a Among Confucius's disciples, Ji Lu (季路, 542–480 BC, also called Zhong You, 仲由, Zi Lu, 子路) was best known for his ability and success in statesmanship. He was noted for his valor and sense of justice, but Confucius often warned him against acting without a second thought.

This is an important aspect of Confucianism. Although it does not deny the existence of supernatural beings, it objects to the worship and study of them and to beliefs concerning the afterlife. Instead, the top priority for humans is to manage well the affairs of life on earth before wasting time on esoteric beliefs and metaphysics. Confucianism emphasizes pragmatism.

13 Min Zi Qian served by Confucius's side in a straightforward and balanced manner. Zi Lu served Confucius in an overconfident and rigid manner. Ran You and Zi Gong served Confucius in a pleasant and joyful manner. Confucius was satisfied with all of them but still warned, "My Zi Lu, beware that your manner could lead you to a tragic death."

13a Zi Lu (子路, 542–480 BC, also known as Zhong You 仲由) was best known for his ability and success in statesmanship. He was, however, noted for his valor and sense of justice. He became a senior official in the state of Wey (衛國) and was later killed during a political upheaval.

Min Zi Qian (閔子騫, 536–487 BC) was a disciple of Confucius and named as one of the twenty-four models of filial piety in the classic *The Book of Filial Piety* (孝經).

Zi You (子有, also known as Ran You, 冉有, Ran Qiu, 冉求 born in 522 BC) was the chief of staff of the Ji Si family and a disciple of Confucius.

Zi Gong (子貢, also known as Duan Mu Ci端木賜, born around 520 BC) was one of the top ten disciples of Confucius. He later became the prime minister of the states of Lu (魯國) and Wey (衛國). He also made a fortune in business and was the wealthiest disciple of Confucius. He advocated making money through propriety, honesty, and trust. His eloquence was also well known. After Confucius's death, Zi Gong observed six years of mourning vigil to show his deep respect for Confucius.

14 The government of the state of Lu (魯國) planned to remodel its treasury building. Min Zi Qian said, "The old building is still in good condition. Why does it need to be remodeled?" Confucius praised Min Zi Qian and said, "He seldom talks but always opens his mouth with substance."

15 Confucius said, "Why did Zhong You's performance on the harp differ from the style of our school?" The other disciples debased Zhong You. Confucius then said, "He is quite proficient already but has not yet reached the master level."

15a Zi Lu (子路, 542–480 BC also known as Zhong You 仲由) was best known for his ability and success in statesmanship. He was however noted for his valor and sense of justice. He became a senior official in the state of Wey (衛國) and was later killed during a political upheaval.

16 Zi Gong asked, "Who is better: Zi Zhang or Zi Xia?" Confucius said, "Zi Zhang is excessive, whereas Zi Xia is inadequate." Zi Gong then said, "Does this mean that Zi Zhang is better than Zi Xia?" Confucius replied, "Being excessive and being inadequate are both faulty."

16a The key sentence here is, "Being excessive and being inadequate are both faulty." This is the main theme of *Zhong Yong* (中庸), *The Book of the Mean* (see endnote 14).

Zi Zhang (子張, 503–447 BC) was a disciple of Confucius.

Zi Xia (子夏, born 507 BC) was a disciple of Confucius and later became an official of the state of Wei (魏國).

17 The wealth of the Ji Si family was more than the duke of Zhou in ancient times. However, Ran Qiu still assisted them to garnish assets from people to further enrich the family. Confucius said, "He does not deserve to be my disciple anymore. You guys can openly criticize him with a trumpet."

17a Ji Kang Zi (季康子, died 468 BC) was the prime minister of the state of Lu (魯國) during the reign of Ai Gong (哀公) and was the most powerful official. His family, the Ji Si family, was a prominent and wealthy family in the state.

Zi You (子有, also known as Ran You, 冉有, Ran Qiu, 冉求 born in 522 BC) was the chief of staff of the Ji Si family and a disciple of Confucius.

The duke of Zhou (周公) was the brother of the founding father of the Zhou Dynasty (周朝).

18 Gao Chai was simple and honest; Zheng Shen was slow; Zhuan Sun Shi was radical; and Zhong You was reckless.

18a Gao Chai (高柴, 521–393 BC) was a disciple of Confucius and had held many official posts. He lived for 128 years.

Zheng Shen (曾参, also known as, Zheng Zi, 曾子, born 505 BC) was a prominent disciple of Confucius, known for his filial piety. He was the author of *The Book of Great Learning* (大學).

Zhuan Sun Shi (顓孫師, 503–447 BC) was a prominent disciple of Confucius.

Zi Lu (子路, 542–480 BC, also known as Zhong You 仲由) was best known for his ability and success in statesmanship. He was, however, noted for his valor and sense of justice. He became a senior official in the state of Wey (衛國) and was later killed during a political upheaval.

19 Confucius said, "Yan Hui was superb in knowledge and morality but was content to live in dire poverty. On the other hand, Duan Mu Ci ignores my teachings and becomes a wealthy businessman. He can often predict accurately the prices of goods."

19a Yan Hui (颜回, also known as Yan Yuan顔淵, 521–481 BC) was Confucius's best disciple. Confucius held him in the highest regard among his disciples.

Duan Mu Ci (端木賜, also known as Zi Gong, 子貢, born around 520 BC) was one of the top ten disciples of Confucius. He later became the prime minister of the states of Lu (魯國) and Wey (衛國). He also made a fortune in business and was the wealthiest disciple of Confucius. He advocated making money through propriety, honesty, and trust. His eloquence was also well known. After Confucius's death, Zi Gong observed six years of mourning vigil to show his deep respect for Confucius.

20 Zi Zhang asked Confucius about the way to be a good person. Confucius said, "If you do not follow the path laid down

by our ancestors, you cannot achieve excellence in knowledge and morality."

21 Confucius said, "You should agree to and endorse a valid argument. However, you must first find out whether the speaker is a Jun Zi or a hypocrite and liar."

21a Jun Zi (君子) is used in Chinese scholarly texts to mean a gentleman, a person of noble character, a prominent and respectable person in society, or a person who upholds virtuous principles.

22 Zi Lu [also known as Zhong You] asked Confucius, "Should I put into action right away what I have learned?" Confucius said, "Since your parents and elder brothers are still alive, how can you put into action right away without consulting them?" Ran You [also known as Ran Qiu] asked Confucius, "Should I put into action right away what I have learned?" Confucius replied, "Sure, put into action." Gong Xi Hua asked Confucius, "When Zi Lu [also known as Zhong You] asked you whether he should act right away, you replied that he should not because his parents and elder brothers were still alive. When Ran You [also known as Ran Qiu] asked the same question, you replied that he should act right away. I am confused. Can you explain?" Confucius replied, "Since Ran Qiu is conservative and timid, I encouraged him to go forward. Since Zhong You is aggressive and overconfident, I advised him to reconsider."

22a Zi Lu (子路, 542–480 BC) was also called Zhong You (仲由). Among Confucius's disciples, he was best known for his ability and success in statesmanship. He was noted for his valor and sense of justice, but Confucius often warned him against acting without a second thought.

Zi You (子有, also known as Ran You, 冉有, Ran Qiu, 冉求 born in 522 BC) was the chief of staff of the Ji Si family and a disciple of Confucius.

Gong Xi Chi (公西赤, born 509 BC, also known as Gong Xi Hua, 公西華) was a disciple of Confucius and was known for his eloquence and diplomatic talents.

This paragraph illustrates that one should not be dogmatic. A doctrine should be applied flexibly depending on the circumstance and the individual character.

23 Confucius and his disciples were captured in the county of Kuang. Yan Yuan was the last one to escape. Confucius spoke to Yan Yuan with a sigh of relief, "I thought you were killed already." Yan Yuan said jokingly, "Master, since you are still alive, how dare I die before you?"

23a The county of Kuang (匡) was once pillaged by Yang Huo (陽貨, also known as Yang Hu 陽虎), a national of the state of Lu (魯國). It so happened that Confucius looked like Yang Huo. When Confucius visited the county, its people mistook Confucius as Yang Huo and captured Confucius together with his disciples.

Yan Hui (颜回, also known as Yan Yuan 顏淵, 521–481 BC) was the best disciple of Confucius. Confucius held him in the highest regard among his disciples.

24 Ji Zi Ran asked whether Zhong You and Ran Qiu could become great ministers. Confucius replied, "I thought you wanted to ask about somebody else. In fact, you want to ask about them. A great minister must be able to serve his king in accordance with propriety and moral principles. He must resign if this is impossible for him to do so. Zhong You and Ran Qiu are ministers but not

necessarily great ministers." Ji Zi Ran asked further, "Would they take their boss's order?" Confucius replied, "If the order is an act of parricide or regicide, they would not take it."

24a Ji Zi Ran (季子然) was a descendant of the prominent and powerful Ji family of the state of Lu (魯國).

Zi Lu (子路, 542–480 BC) was also called Zhong You (仲由). Among Confucius's disciples, he was best known for his ability and success in statesmanship. He was noted for his valor and sense of justice, but Confucius often warned him against acting without a second thought.

Zi You (子有, also known as Ran You, 冉有, Ran Qiu, 冉求 born in 522 BC) was the chief of staff of the Ji Si family and a disciple of Confucius.

25 Zi Lu appointed the young Zi Kao to be the governor of the county of Fei in the state of Lu (魯國). Confucius said to Zi Lu, "You are ruining somebody's son." Zi Lu argued, "That place has an established society with civilized people. Why does he need to be educated before taking on the job? He can learn on the job." Confucius said, "I don't like people who argue eloquently but cunningly."

26 Zi Lu, Zheng Xi, Ran You, and Gong Xi Hua sat beside Confucius.

Confucius said, "I am a bit older than you guys. Therefore, you can speak up freely. You often said that I do not understand you. Suppose that I understand you. What do you want to accomplish in life?"

Zi Lu [also known as Zhong You] spoke up first and replied, "I wish I could be a leader of a country with a thousand chariots [a country of decent size], which is dominated and surrounded by large countries and is under the threat of military confrontation, resulting in poverty and famine. I want to turn it around in three years so that it will emerge strong."

Confucius smiled and turned to Ran Qiu [also known as Ran You] and asked, "How about you?"

Ran Qiu replied, "I would not mind leading a small country with sixty to seventy square miles or even fifty to sixty square miles in size. I hope that, in three years, I could bring prosperity to its people. As for the fostering of the principles of Li and promotion of music, I would wait for the advent of a Jun Zi to get the job done."

Confucius then turned to Gong Xi Hua and asked, "Chi, how about you?"

Gong Xi Hua [also known as Gong Xi Chi] replied, "I dare not say I am competent, but I will try to learn. During the services of the worship of the king's ancestors or a royal reception of foreign diplomats, I hope I can be a junior attending official, dressed up in official attire."

Confucius then turned to Zheng Xi and asked, "Dian, how about you?"

Zheng Xi was playing his harpsichord when Confucius asked. He immediately tuned down the music, stopped playing, stood up, and said, "My ambition is different from my other three colleagues."

Confucius said, "It won't hurt talking about each one's ambition openly and freely."

Zheng Xi then said, "I dream of a day in late spring when I put on a new spring dress, hang out with a group of five to six adult friends and six to seven children, bathe in the river, dance in the breeze and under the clouds, sing songs, recite poems, and then return home."

Confucius lamented, "I am with you too!"

After the other three disciples left the room, Zheng Xi stayed behind and asked Confucius, "What do you think about the wishes of the other three guys?"

Confucius said, "Not much. They are just casual discussions about their own ambition."

Zheng Xi then asked, "Why did you smile at Zhong You?"

Confucius said, "The foundation of the governance of a country is the principle of Li (禮). Since Zhong You was not humble enough, I smiled at him."

Zheng Xi asked, "Was the territory spoken of by Ran Qiu a country already?"

Confucius said, "Yes. Why is a territory of that size not a country?"

Zheng Xi asked, "Was the territory spoken of by Gong Xi Hua a country already?"

Confucius said, "Of course. It is a significant country already because it has established official worships of regal ancestors and diplomatic relationships with other countries. If Gong Xi Hua is just a junior official there, who can have the caliber and qualifications to be a senior official in that country?"

26a Zi Lu (子路, 542–480 BC) was also called Zhong You (仲由). Among Confucius's disciples, he was best known for his ability and success in statesmanship. He was noted for his valor and sense of justice, but Confucius often warned him against acting without a second thought.

Zheng Xi (曾晳, also known as Zheng Dian, 曾點) was a disciple of Confucius.

Zi You (子有, also known as Ran You, 冉有, Ran Qiu, 冉求 born in 522 BC) was the chief of staff of the Ji Si family and a disciple of Confucius.

Gong Xi Chi (公西赤, born 509 BC, also known as Gong Xi Hua公西華) was a disciple of Confucius and was known for his eloquence and diplomatic talents.

CHAPTER 12

YAN YUAN (顏淵)

1 Yan Yuan asked about the essence of Ren. Confucius replied, "Control yourself so that your words and behavior are in line with the principles of Li (禮). If you can do so in the future, people around the world will emulate you and follow the path to Ren virtue. It is all up to you to have the Ren virtue. Nobody else can help or deter you." Yan Yuan asked further, "Can you please tell me the key points?" Confucius said, "Don't look at anything that is against the principles of Li; don't listen to any matter that is against the principles of Li; don't talk about any matter that is against the principles of Li; don't take any action that is against the principles of Li." Yan Yuan said, "Although I am not quite intelligent, I get it. I will follow your teaching."

1a The word *Ren* (仁) in Confucianism embodies all the core virtues of humanity, including love. It can be translated into "humaneness" and "benevolence" as a proxy. Since it cannot be translated precisely to a single English word, the Chinese pronunciation *Ren* is used here and in the following translation (see endnote 3).

The word *Li* (禮) in Confucianism and in the Chinese language in general has many meanings. In ancient times, it referred to rites, rituals, ceremonies, protocols in courts and government, discipline, regulations, laws and order, respect, courtesy, and etiquette in daily life; in modern times, it refers to respect, etiquette, courtesy, presents, and gifts. Li (禮) includes a set of social norms that are motivated by the inner conscience of people and entrenched in the culture rather than externally imposed by the government through decrees and legislation (see endnote 7).

2 Zhong Gong asked about the essence of Ren virtue. Confucius explained, "Whenever you step outside your home, you always behave as if you are meeting an important person. When you direct your people, you take it seriously as if you are handling a big ceremonial event. You do not impose on others what you dislike. You cause no grief in your country as well as at home." Zhong Gong said, "Although I am not that intelligent, I get it and will follow your advice."

2a Ran Yong (冉雍, born 522 BC, also known as 仲弓Zhong Gong) was a prominent disciple of Confucius.

Many religions in the world preach the same principle: "You do not impose on others what you dislike."

3 Si Ma Niu asked about the essence of Ren virtue. Confucius said, "People who have Ren virtue tend to be reserved and cautious in their words." Si Ma Niu then commented, "Does Ren virtue involve just being reserved and cautious in words?" Confucius said, "Since practicing the Ren virtue is very demanding, how can one not be reserved and cautious in words and brag about his virtue?"

3a Some scholars believed that Si Ma Niu (司馬牛), a disciple of Confucius, had a brother Huan Tui (桓魋) who was a powerful and notorious chief of army of the state of Song (宋國).

4 Si Ma Niu asked about Jun Zi. Confucius said, "A Jun Zi does not worry and fear." Si Ma Niu then asked, "Having no worry and fear? Is that enough to be a Jun Zi?" Confucius said, "If upon reflection, one has no regrets in his conscience, what worry and what fear does he have?"

5 Si Ma Niu lamented, "Everybody has brothers—except me." Zi Xia comforted him, "I have heard that life and death are determined by fate; wealth and poverty are determined by heaven. If a Jun Zi acts seriously and properly, he will not make mistakes. If a Jun Zi behaves respectfully according to the principles of Li, everyone in the world is your brother. Therefore, a Jun Zi is never afraid of having no brother."

5a Some scholars believed that Si Ma Niu (司馬牛), a disciple of Confucius, had a brother Huan Tui (桓魋) who was a powerful and notorious chief army commander of the state of Song (宋國). Si Ma Niu denounced his brother. Therefore, he said that he had no brother.

Zi Xia (子夏, born 507 BC) was a disciple of Confucius and later became an official of the state of Wei (魏國).

6 Zi Zhang asked about what constitutes wisdom. Confucius said, "If you are not bothered by covert slanders like water seeping gradually through damp walls or overt smears like cutting your skin, you are indeed wise. If you are not bothered by covert slanders like water seeping gradually through damp walls or overt smears like cutting your skin, your wisdom is beyond common people by far."

6a Zi Zhang (子張, 503–447 BC) was a disciple of Confucius.

7 Zi Gong asked about good governance. Confucius said, "Food abundance, strong army, trust and approval by people." Zi

Gong asked, "If we must eliminate one of the three, which one should be eliminated first?" Confucius said, "Eliminate strong army." Zi Gong asked further, "If we must eliminate two of the three, which two should be eliminated?" Confucius said, "Eliminate food abundance. Death is an eventuality anyhow. A country will collapse if its government lacks the trust and support of its people."

8 Ji Zi Cheng said, "What matters for a Jun Zi are his internal qualities. Why should one bother with exterior grace and appearance?" Zi Gong said, "I am sorry to hear that about a Jun Zi, sir. Once words are uttered from the mouth, they are like chariots carried by four horses. They cannot be retracted easily. Exterior grace and appearance depend on internal qualities. Likewise, internal qualities are inseparable from exterior appearance. Take for example the hides of tigers and leopards. If we pull out the hair of such hides, they are not different from the hides of dogs and lambs."

8a Ji Zi Cheng (棘子成) was a minister of the state of Wey (衛國).

Zi Gong (子貢, also known as Duan Mu Ci端木賜, born around 520 BC) was one of the top ten disciples of Confucius. He later became the prime minister of the states of Lu (魯國) and Wey (衛國). He also made a fortune in business and was the wealthiest disciple of Confucius. He advocated making money through propriety, honesty, and trust. His eloquence was also well known. After Confucius's death, Zi Gong observed six years of mourning vigil to show his deep respect for Confucius.

9 Ai Gong asked You Ruo, "Our country is suffering from a famine. The treasury coffers are running out. What should I do?" You Ruo replied, "Have you lowered the income tax rate to 10 percent?" Ai Gong said, "The tax rate is already 20 percent now, and it is still not enough for the country. If I lowered it to 10 percent,

how can I make ends meet?" You Ruo replied, "If your people have more disposable income, how can the country be in deficit? If your people are poor, how can the country have a surplus?"

9a Ai Gong (哀公) was the duke of Lu (魯國) from 494 to 468 BC.

You Zi (有子, also known as You Ruo 有若, born around 518 BC) was a student of Confucius.

You Ruo's theory superseded a modern theory on taxation: the higher the taxes the country imposes on people, the poorer its people will be. In turn, the national income will drop, resulting in an impoverished country.

10 Zi Zhang asked how to excel in morality and how to avoid delusion. Confucius said, "Loyalty, honesty, and righteousness are the keys to the highest standard of morality. You want your loved ones to live and hated ones to die. If you are inconsistent and vacillate, you are deluded. *The Book of Poetry* has a verse: 'I don't care about his wealth; I care that he is unfaithful.'"

10a Zi Zhang (子張, 503–447 BC) was a disciple of Confucius.

11 Duke Jing of Qi asked Confucius how to run a government. Confucius said, "The king should fulfill his responsibilities as a king; ministers should fulfill their responsibilities as ministers; fathers [parents] should fulfill their responsibilities as fathers [parents]; children should fulfill their responsibilities as children." The duke said, "You are absolutely correct. When the king fails to fulfill his responsibilities as a king, ministers fail to fulfill their responsibilities as ministers, fathers fail to fulfill their responsibilities as fathers, children fail to fulfill their responsibilities as children, even if I

have a huge amount of food, I might not be able to eat it [because I might be killed]!"

11a Duke Jing (齊景公) was the duke of Qi (齊國), a large hegemon during the Spring-Autumn Period.

12 Confucius said, "Zhong You is the person who can make a judgment a lawsuit based on one-sided arguments." Zi Lu always kept his promise before the day was over.

12a Zi Lu (子路, 542–480 BC also known as Zhong You 仲由) was best known for his ability and success in statesmanship. He was noted for his valor and sense of justice.

13 Confucius said, "During a legal litigation, we are no different from anybody [all are equal]. The best strategy is to avoid a litigation as far as possible."

14 Zi Zhang asked about how to run a government. Confucius said, "You should work tirelessly on your official job and be loyal to your mandate and mission."

15 Confucius said, "If you broaden your knowledge and restraint yourself according to principles of Li, you will not be devious."

16 Confucius said, "A Jun Zi helps others realize their good dreams and avoids abetting others' demise. A Xiao Ren does the opposite."

16a Jun Zi (君子) in Chinese scholarly texts means a gentleman, a person of noble character, a prominent and respectable person in society, or a person who upholds virtuous principles.

A Xiao Ren (小人) is a person with the opposite characteristics of a Jun Zi. A Xiao Ren is, for example, mean, wicked, cruel, dumb, and/or lacking in virtues.

17 Ji Kang Zi asked Confucius about good governance. Confucius replied, "Governance means propriety. If Your Honor follows propriety, who dares behave improperly?"

17a Ji Kang Zi (季康子, died 468 BC) was the prime minister of the state of Lu (魯國) during the reign of Ai Gong (哀公) and was the most powerful official.

18 Ji Kang Zi was worried about the large number of larcenies and robberies in his country and asked Confucius what to do. Confucius said, "Given that Your Honor is not greedy and corrupted, even if such crimes are rewarding, your people will not commit such crimes."

18a Ji Kang Zi (季康子) was a powerful but malicious and an unpopular prime minister of the state of Lu (魯國).

19 Ji Kang Zi asked Confucius about governance, "If we kill all unruly people, we will be left with all compliant citizens. How about such idea?" Confucius replied, "Your Honor, why do you need to kill people to maintain good governance? If you set your mind toward meritorious deeds, your people will also be meritorious. The morality of the king [leader] is like wind, and the morality of the citizenry is like grass. When wind blows over grass, it must bend with the wind."

20 Zi Zhang asked, "What will make a person accomplished?" Confucius said, "Why do you ask this? What do you mean by being accomplished?" Zi Zhang replied, "Being famous in the country and also famous in the family." Confucius said, "Being famous is

not the same as being accomplished. An accomplished person has an upright character and is committed to righteousness. He listens carefully and pays attention to others' body language. He cares about his subordinates. Such a person will be accomplished in his country and family. On the other hand, a famous person appears to have Ren virtues but acts against them behind the scenes. He is not ashamed to publicize his fake virtues. Such a person will be famous in his country and family."

21 Fan Chi accompanied Confucius for a walk under the rain altar and asked, "May I ask about how to excel in virtue, repent sins, and discern delusion?" Confucius said, "Good questions indeed! If you focus on doing good work first and put aside its potential reward to you, is that an example of excellence in virtue? If you are critical of your own shortcomings and do not criticize others' shortcomings, is that an example of repentance? If you act out of animus with the consequence of hurting yourself and your loved ones, is that an example of delusion?"

21a A rain altar was a terrace where the king or ruler of the country prayed for the appropriate abundance of rain for the crops. In an agricultural society, an abundance of rain was important.

Fan Chi (樊遲, born about 505 BC) was a prominent disciple of Confucius. He followed Confucius's footsteps and became a teacher of Confucianism.

22 Fan Chi asked about Ren virtue. Confucius said, "Love people." Fan Chi then asked about wisdom. Confucius said, "Understand people." Fan Chi did not get it. Confucius said, "You appoint and promote upright people and ignore and demote wicked people, so that wickedness will be replaced by righteousness." After Fan Chi left, he met Zi Xia and said, "A moment ago, I asked Confucius about wisdom. Confucius talked about appointing and

promoting upright people and ignoring and demoting wicked people, so that wickedness will be replaced by righteousness. What does this mean?" Zi Xia said, "This indeed has a deep meaning. In the old days, when Shun became the emperor, he appointed Gao Yao as the prime minister among many candidates. As a result, wicked people left. When Tang became the emperor, he appointed Yi Yin as the prime minister among many candidates. As a result, wicked people left."

22a Shun (舜, 2294–2184 BC) was the emperor of the ancient utopian period in China.

Gao Yao (皋陶, 2220–2113 BC) was the prime minister for Shun and was regarded as a great ruler, politician, and philosopher by later scholars.

Tang (湯, 1670–1587 BC) was the founding emperor of the Shang Dynasty (商朝)).

Yi Yin (伊尹, 1649–1550 BC) was the prime minister for Tang and was regarded as a great ruler, politician, and philosopher by later scholars.

23 Zi Gong asked about how to deal with a friend. Confucius said, "Give good advice and guidance. If this does not work, stop nagging. Don't embarrass yourself."

24 Zheng Zi said, "A Jun Zi makes friends on the basis of common interests in literature and knowledge and relies on friendship to enhance his Ren virtue."

24a Zheng Zi (曾子, also known as Zheng Shen曾參, born 505 BC) was a prominent disciple of Confucius, known for his filial piety. He was the author of *The Book of Great Learning* (大學).

CHAPTER 13

ZI LU (子路)

1 Zi Lu asked about good governance. Confucius said, "Lead your people by education and enlightenment and induce them to work hard." Zi Lu asked for further elaboration. Confucius said, "Do these relentlessly."

2 Zhong Gong became the chief of staff of the Ji family and asked Confucius about governance. Confucius said, "You must first lay out clearly the mandates and responsibilities of your staff. You forgive their minor mistakes. You appoint and promote competent and meritorious candidates." Zhong Gong then asked, "How do I identify competent and meritorious candidates so I can appoint and promote them?" Confucius said, "Appoint and promote those based on your knowledge of them. For those whom you do not know, would other people ignore them?"

2a Ran Yong (冉雍, born 522 BC, also known as 仲弓Zhong Gong) was a prominent disciple of Confucius.

3 Zi Lu spoke to Confucius, "The duke of Wey wants to hire you to help him govern his country. What steps would you take first?" Confucius said, "I would first ask him to announce my official title." Zi Lu said, "Are you too demanding? Why is a proper title

so important?" Confucius said, "You are unsophisticated indeed, Zhong You! A Jun Zi always gives the benefit of the doubt to matters unknown to him. If the official title is inappropriate, I will not have the clout to talk openly and freely. If I cannot talk openly and freely, I cannot accomplish my mandates and goals. If I cannot accomplish my mandates and goals, I cannot promote Li and music [social norms and good culture]. If Li and music are not widely accepted, it will be difficult to establish law and order. If law and order are not established, the people will be disoriented. Therefore, a Jun Zi must have a proper title so that he has the clout to talk freely and give orders. When a Jun Zi talks, his words should carry weight."

3a Zi Lu (子路, 542–480 BC), also called Zhong You (仲由), was a disciple of Confucius and was best known for his ability and success in statesmanship. He was also noted for his valor and sense of justice.

Jun Zi in the last sentence means a high-ranking official. This paragraph delineated the sequence of good governance according to Confucius: (1) clear mandate, (2) freedom of speech, (3) social norms and culture, (4) law and order, (5) good citizenry.

4 Fan Chi asked Confucius to teach him farming. Confucius said, "I am not as good as an old farmer." Fan Chi later asked Confucius to teach him gardening. Confucius said, "I am not as good as an old gardener." Fan Chi left, disappointed. Confucius said, "Fan Chi is narrow-minded indeed! If the leader cherishes Li (禮), his people will not be disrespectful to him. If the leader cherishes righteousness and honor, his people will not be disobedient. If the leader cherishes honesty and trust, his people will not be aloof. If his does so, people from all over the world will come with their babies and toddlers and join his country. Why does he need to learn farming and gardening?"

5 Confucius said, "Some scholars can recite three hundred odes, but when they are entrusted with running a government, they fail in their mandate. When they are sent as envoys to other countries, they fail in their diplomatic assignments. Although their literary knowledge is immense, what use can they be?"

6 Confucius said, "If a leader's personal conduct is righteous and proper, his people will carry out his order even without an explicit decree. If a leader's personal conduct is improper, his people will not follow his order explicitly decreed."

7 Confucius said, "The governments of the state of Lu and the state of Wey are like brothers."

7a The state of Lu (鲁國) and the state of Wey (衛國) were two small states during the Spring-Autumn Period.

8 Confucius said of Prince Jing of the state of Wey, "He manages his personal finances well. Before he started to build his wealth, he said: 'I am satisfied with what I have.' After his wealth had grown a little bit, he said: 'I have enough.' After he had become very wealthy, he said, 'That is beautiful.'"

9 Confucius visited the state of Wey, and Ran You acted as the driver of his carriage. Confucius observed, "Its people are numerous indeed!" Ran You then asked, "Given that they have a big population, what else should be done for them?" Confucius replied, "Enrich them." Ran You asked further, "After they are enriched, what else should be done for them?" Confucius said, "Educate them."

9a Zi You (子有, also known as Ran You, 冉有, Ran Qiu, 冉求 born in 522 BC) was the chief of staff of the Ji Si family and a disciple of Confucius.

10 Confucius said, "If I were employed to run a government, I could make a difference in twelve months and a major accomplishment in three years."

11 Confucius said, "If a country is governed by good leadership for a hundred years, violence can be eradicated, and capital punishment can be dispensed with. True indeed is this saying."

12 Confucius said, "Even if a country has a great leader who rules it according to Ren principles, he will still require thirty years for such principles to flourish in the country."

13 Confucius said, "If a leader's personal conduct is righteous and proper, what difficulty will he have in running the government? If he cannot rectify himself, how can he rectify others?"

14 Ran Qiu returned home after a royal court session. Confucius asked him, "Why are you so late?" Ran Qiu replied, "Lots of government affairs." Confucius said, "They must be affairs of the Ji family. If these are government affairs, I would like to know about them even though I am not an official."

14a Zi You (子有, also known as Ran You, 冉有, Ran Qiu, 冉求 born in 522 BC) was the chief of staff of the Ji Si family and a disciple of Confucius.

15 Lu Ding Gong asked Confucius, "There is a saying that one spoken sentence can uplift a country. Is this real?" Confucius replied, "We cannot expect too much from just one sentence. A proverb says: 'It is difficult to be a ruler of a country, and it is not easy to be a minister as well.' Since we know that it is difficult to be a ruler, how is it possible to uplift a country with just one sentence?" Lu Ding Gong then asked, "There is a saying that one spoken sentence can ruin a country. Is this real?" Confucius replied, "We cannot expect

too much from just one sentence. A proverb says: 'There is no fun to be a ruler, except that nobody dares to oppose his words.' If the ruler's words are good and his people dare not oppose them, is this desirable indeed? If the ruler's words are bad and nobody dares to oppose them, would the words of the ruler ruin the country?"

15a Lu Ding Gong (鲁定公) was the duke of Lu (鲁国) from 509 to 495 BC.

16 Ye Gong asked about politics. Confucius said, "Foster happiness to your neighbors and welcome foreigners from afar."

16a Ye Gong (葉公, born 529 BC) was a prime minister of the state of Chu (楚国).

17 Zi Xia became the governor of the county of Ju Fu. He consulted Confucius about how to run a government. Confucius said, "Don't rush. Do not focus on trivial benefits. If you rush, you will not reach your goals. If you care about trivial benefits, major undertakings will not be accomplished."

17a Ju Fu (莒父) was a county inside the state of Lu (鲁国).

Zi Xia (子夏, born 507 BC) was a disciple of Confucius and later became an official of the state of Wei (魏国).

18 Ye Gong told Confucius, "There is an upright person in my clan who testified against his father for stealing a lamb." Confucius said, "Upright people in my clan behave differently. The fathers do not testify against their children and vice versa. This is how they view righteousness."

18a Ye Gong (葉公, born 529 BC) was a prime minister of the state of Chu (楚国).

19 Fan Chi asked about Ren virtues. Confucius said, "You behave respectfully at home, handle your work seriously, and deal with others with loyalty and sincerity. Do not relinquish these principles even when you are in a barbaric place."

19a Fan Chi (樊遲, born about 505 BC) was a prominent disciple of Confucius.

20 Zi Gong asked, "What qualities must one have to entitle him to be called an intellectual and honorable official?" Confucius said, "He must conduct himself with a sense of shame. When he is sent as an envoy to other countries, he must not disgrace his mission. If he can do so, he deserves to be called an intellectual and honorable official." Zi Gong then asked, "May I ask what qualities are secondary?" Confucius said, "He must be praised for being filial to his clan and for being brotherly with his fellow men." Zi Gong asked further, "What is next?" Confucius said, "He talks honestly, keeps his promises, and follows through with his actions. However, even some Xiao Rens can do so! Even so, these are still good secondary qualities." Zi Gong then asked, "How about the existing officials in our government?" Confucius responded, "Oh! These minions do not deserve our discussion."

21 Confucius said, "It is difficult to find and befriend people who practice the principles of Zhong Yong. Some are too aggressive, whereas some are too conservative. The aggressive type is proactive and progressive, whereas the conservative type is timid and retroactive."

21a Zhong Yong (中庸) is the central doctrine of Confucianism. Confucius's grandson Zi Si (子思) wrote *The Book of Zhong Yong* (*The Book of the Mean*).

Zhong means unbiased, not in excess in one way or the other, nothing more and nothing less. Yong means ordinary, commonplace, firm, unwavering, and perpetual truth (see endnote 14).

22 Confucius said, "Southerners have a proverb: 'A person without dedication and constancy cannot become a witch doctor.' It is very true!" *The Book of Changes* [*I Ching*] has a sentence that says: 'Not upholding constantly one's virtues will lead to shame.' Confucius said, "One does not need to consult the oracles since the consequence is predictable."

23 Confucius said, "A Jun Zi has independent opinions but can resolve differences in opinions harmoniously. On the other hand, a Xiao Ren shows consensus in appearance but is contentious underneath."

Or:

Confucius said, "A Jun Zi is affable but does not join gangs. On the other hand, a Xiao Ren joins gangs but is contentious underneath."

23a Jun Zi (君子) is a gentleman, a person of noble character, a prominent and respectable person in society, or a person who upholds virtuous principles.

A Xiao Ren (小人) is a person with the opposite characteristics of a Jun Zi. A Xiao Ren is, for example, mean, wicked, cruel, dumb and/or lacking in virtues.

24 Zi Gong asked, "If all my fellow men love me, am I good enough?" Confucius said, "Not yet." Zi Gong then asked, "If all my fellow men hate me, am I bad?" Confucius said, "Not necessarily.

You want ideally that only good fellow men love you and only bad fellow men hate you."

24a Zi Gong (子貢, also known as Duan Mu Ci端木賜, born around 520 BC) was one of the top ten disciples of Confucius. He later became the prime minister of the states of Lu (魯國) and Wey (衛國). He also made a fortune in business and was the wealthiest disciple of Confucius. He advocated making money through propriety, honesty, and trust. His eloquence was also well known. After Confucius's death, Zi Gong observed six years of mourning vigil to show his deep respect for Confucius.

25 Confucius said, "It is easy to work with a Jun Zi but difficult to please him. He cannot be pleased by improper means. He respects and values the capability of his staff. A Xiao Ren is difficult to work with but is easy to please. He can be pleased by improper means. He is overcritical and demanding on his staff."

25a Jun Zi (君子) is a gentleman, a person of noble character, a prominent and respectable person in society, or a person who upholds virtuous principles.

A Xiao Ren (小人) is a person with the opposite characteristics of a Jun Zi. A Xiao Ren is, for example, mean, wicked, cruel, dumb and/or lacking in virtues.

26 Confucius said, "A Jun Zi has peace of mind and is not arrogant. A Xiao Ren is arrogant and has no peace of mind."

27 Confucius said, "The combination of firmness, perseverance, simplicity, and modesty is close to the Ren virtue."

28 Zi Lu asked, "How can I become an elite scholar?" Confucius said, "If you participate in mutual and constructive criticisms,

collaborate in intellectual exchanges, and behave amicably, you will become an elite scholar. You participate in mutual and constructive criticisms with friends. You behave amicably among your brothers."

28a Zi Lu (子路, 542–480 BC also known as Zhong You, 仲由) was best known for his ability and success in statesmanship. He was noted for his valor and sense of justice.

29 Confucius said, "After people have been trained for seven years by a competent person, they can then be sent to fight in a war."

30 Confucius said, "Sending untrained soldiers to war is equivalent to sacrificing them."

CHAPTER 14

YUAN XIAN ASKED (憲問)

1 Yuan Xian asked about shame. Confucius said, "If the government of a country is good and clean, and you collect a salary as an official, and if the government is corrupt and decadent, and you still collect a salary as an official, shame on you." Yuan Xian then asked, "If one can repress the vices of abrasiveness, boasting, resentment and bitterness, greed and indulgence, can he be deemed to have Ren virtue?" Confucius said, "He is indeed exceptionally outstanding, but I am not sure whether he has Ren virtue yet."

1a Yuan Xian (原憲, also known as Yuan Si, 原思 and Zi Si, 子思, born 515 BC) was a disciple of Confucius.

2 Confucius said, "If a scholar cherishes comfort at home, he does not deserve to be a scholar."

3 Confucius said, "When the government of your country is good, you can talk assertively and act boldly. When the government of your country is corrupt, you still can act boldly, but your words need to be reserved and cautious."

4 Confucius said, "A virtuous person would definitely talk about his lofty ideals. However, those who talk about lofty ideals are not necessarily virtuous. Those who have Ren virtue must be brave. However, brave people do not necessarily have Ren virtue."

5 Nan Gong Kuo spoke with Confucius and said, "The legendary Yi was skillful in archery, and Ao could tow a boat with his bare hands. However, both had tragic deaths. On the other hand, Yu of the Xia Dynasty and Ji in ancient times toiled in the fields. Yet they eventually became founders of their empires." Confucius kept quiet. After Nan Gong Kuo left, Confucius said, "He is a Jun Zi and a virtuous person indeed."

5a Nan Gong Kuo (南宮适, also known as Nan Rong 南容) was married to the niece of Confucius and was a disciple of Confucius.

In the legend, Yi (羿) was the duke of a small country and known for his archery. He was ultimately killed by another king in a struggle for power.

Ao (奡) was a giant. He could lift and tow a big boat with his bare hands. He was also killed by his rival.

Great Yu (禹, around 2237–2139 BC) was the founder of the Xia Dynasty (夏朝). He was regarded by historians to be a saintly king.

Ji (稷) was a legendary leader in prehistorical times. He introduced farming and taught his people husbandry.

6 Confucius said, "There are some Jun Zi who may not have Ren virtue. There are no Xiao Ren who have Ren virtue."

6a Jun Zi (君子) is a gentleman, a person of noble character, a prominent and respectable person in society, or a person who upholds virtuous principles.

A Xiao Ren (小人) is a person with the opposite characteristics of a Jun Zi. A Xiao Ren is, for example, mean, wicked, cruel, dumb and/or lacking in virtues.

7 Confucius said, "If you love a person, can you not drill him and let him toil? If you are loyal to a person, can you not counsel and admonish him?"

8 Confucius said, "The state of Zheng formulates a decree in the following steps: Pi Shen first prepared the draft, which was then reviewed and discussed by Shi Shu, edited by the foreign policy minister, Zi Yu, and finally polished by the prime minister, Zi Chan, from the East Village."

8a Pi Shen (裨諶) was a low-level minister from the state of Zheng (鄭國).

Shi Shu (世叔) was another minister from the state of Zheng. He became the prime minister after Zi Chan.

Zi Yu (子羽) was the minister responsible for foreign affairs of the state of Zheng.

Zi Chan (子產, died 552 BC, also known as Gong Sun Qiao 公孫僑) was a prominent statesman and reputed prime minister of the state of Zheng (鄭國).

9 Someone asked about Zi Chan. Confucius commented, "He was a charitable and benevolent man." That person further asked about Zi Si. Confucius exclaimed, "Oh, that guy! That guy!" That

person then asked about Guan Zhong. Confucius said, "He was a capable man. He confiscated a city of three hundred households from Bo Si, which was originally bestowed on Bo Si by the duke of Qi. As a result, Bo Si had to live in poverty, eating coarse rice until his death. Yet Bo Si did not resent."

9a Zi Chan (子產, died 552 BC, also known as Gong Sun Qiao 公孫僑) was a prominent statesman and reputed prime minister of the state of Zheng (鄭國).

Zi Si (子西) was the prime minister of the state of Chu (楚國).

Bo Shi (伯氏) was a minister of the state of Qi (齊國).

Guan Zhong (管仲, 725–645 BC) was a prominent politician, philosopher, and pioneer of the School of Law (Legalism) before Confucius and was a dominant minister of the state of Qi (齊國). He helped the state of Qi become a hegemon. He advocated the implementation of tough laws and promotion of commerce for the country.

10 Confucius said, "It is difficult for a poor person to feel no resentment and bitterness. It is easier for a wealthy person to stay away from extravagance and arrogance."

10a This sentence has a far-reaching implication to governance and politics of the masses.

11 Confucius said, "Meng Gong Chuo is more than qualified to be the chief of staff (butler) of the houses of Zhao and Wei. He should not become a minister of the state of Teng or Xue."

11a Meng Gong Chuo (孟公綽) was a minister of the state of Lu (鲁國). He was known for his austere lifestyle and honesty. He was highly praised by Confucius.

The house of Zhao was the royal family of the state of Zhao (趙國), which was a large state.

The house of Wei was the royal family of the state of Wei (魏國), which was another large state.

The state of Teng (滕國) and the state of Xue (薛國) were tiny states.

12 Zi Lu asked what constituted a perfect man. Confucius said, "If the person is as knowledgeable as Zang Wu Zhong, as uncovetous as Meng Gong Chuo, as brave as Bian Zhuang Zi, as dexterous as Ran Qiu, and is polished with Li and music, he can be deemed to be a perfect man." Confucius also said, "However, today's perfect man may not reach such high standards. If he remains righteous in view of a gainful opportunity, is willing to sacrifice his life during a crisis, and never forgets his promises and vows, he can be deemed to be a perfect man."

12a Zang Wu Zhong (臧武仲) was a prime minister of the state of Lu (鲁國) before Confucius's time. He was known to be knowledgeable.

Meng Gong Chuo (孟公綽) was a minister of the state of Lu (鲁國). He was known for his austere lifestyle and honesty. He was highly praised by Confucius.

Bian Zhuang Zi (卞莊子) was a minister of the state of Lu (鲁國) before Confucius's time. He was known to be a master of martial arts and a great warrior. There was a legend that he killed two tigers after they fought over their prey. The bigger tiger was wounded, and the smaller tiger was defeated and maimed. Bian Zhuang watched their fight, waited, and then killed the wounded tiger with his knife before he slaughtered the dying one. This story was labeled in Chinese history as "Bian Zhuang Killing Tigers."

Zi You (子有, also known as Ran You, 冉有, Ran Qiu, 冉求 born in 522 BC) was the chief of staff of the Ji Si (季氏) family and a disciple of Confucius.

13 Confucius asked Gong Ming Jia about Gong Shu Wen Zi, "Some people say that your master does not talk, does not laugh, and does not take from people. Is this true?" Gong Ming Jia replied, "That is just an exaggeration. My master only talks when it is the right time to talk, so others are not annoyed by him. He laughs only when he is joyful, so others are not annoyed by his laughter. He takes when it is appropriate for him to take, so others are not bothered by his taking." Confucius said, "Really? Is that really true?"

13a Gong Shu Wen Zi (公叔文子) was a minister of the state of Wey (衛國).

Gong Ming Jia (公明賈) worked for Gong Shu Wen Zi.

14 Confucius said, "Zang Wu Zhong used the city of Fang as a bargaining chip to entice the duke of Lu to bestow his son, Zang Wei, to be a minister and inherit the estate of his family. Although some people said that he did not twist the arms of the duke, I do not think so."

14a Zang Wu Zhong (臧武仲) was a prime minister of the state of Lu (魯國) before Confucius's time. He was known to be knowledgeable.

The city of Fang (防) was bestowed on Zang Wu Zhong by the duke of Lu when Zang was appointed prime minister. Therefore, it was supposed to be part of his estate. Zang later lost a political fight with another powerful minister, Meng Sun Si (孟孫氏), who dominated the court of the state. Zang escaped from the state for a while. He later returned to the city, occupied, and repossessed it without official permission. He did not want to relinquish his ownership of the city. He negotiated with the duke that, if his son, Zang Wei (臧為), was appointed to be a minister and his legal heir, he would relinquish the city. Confucius thought that Zang's request was licentious. Zang should have returned the city to the duke before asking for another favor.

Zang was regarded by Confucius to be learned and intelligent. However, being learned and intelligent was insufficient for Ren virtue.

15 Confucius said, "Wen Gong of Jin was crafty and not upright. Huan Gong of Qi was upright and not crafty."

15a Wen Gong of Jin (晉文公, 671–628 BC) was the duke of Jin (晉國), one of the five prominent hegemons during the Spring-Autumn Period.

Huan Gong of Qi (齊桓公, 725–643 BC) was the duke of Qi (齊國), the top among the five hegemons during the Spring-Autumn Period. He was highly respected by all feudal rulers.

16 Zi Lu said, "Qi Huan Gong killed his brother Prince Jiu. His supporter Shao Hu committed suicide in protest, whereas Guan Zhong did not die." Zi Lu then asked, "Did Guan Zhong have Ren virtue?" Confucius said, "Huan Gong was able to repeatedly form and lead an alliance of all the feudal kings and lords without the deployment of one soldier or one chariot. Such success was due to the

effort and contribution of Guan Zhong. He has Ren virtue indeed! He is virtuous indeed!"

16a Qi Huan Gong (齊桓公, 725–643 BC) was the duke of Qi (齊國), the top among the five hegemons during the Spring-Autumn Period. He was highly respected by all feudal rulers.

Prince Jiu (公子纠) was the elder brother of Qi Huan Gong. The two brothers contended for the throne. During the struggle, Prince Jiu was killed by Qi Huan Gong. Both Shao Hu (召忽) and Guan Zhong (管仲) were originally on the staff of Prince Jiu. After Prince Jiu was killed, Shao Hu committed suicide by jumping into an abyss in protest to show his loyalty to Prince Jiu. However, Guan Zhong defected and joined Qi Huan Gong as his prime minister.

Guan Zhong (管仲, 725–645 BC) was a prominent politician, philosopher, and pioneer of the School of Law (Legalism) before Confucius and was a dominant minister of the state of Qi (齊國). He helped the state of Qi become a hegemon. He advocated the implementation of tough laws and promotion of commerce for the country.

17 Zi Gong said, "I don't think that Guan Zhong had Ren virtue. After Qi Huan Gong killed Prince Jiu, Guan Zhong did not die with him but rather became the prime minister for Qi Huan Gong." Confucius said, "Guan Zhong assisted Qi Huan Gong to become the head hegemon of all the feudal rulers so that peace in the whole world has lasted until today. We are still getting the benefits of his great achievements. Without Guan Zhong, we would be barbarians and would dress in rags. We should not expect him to act like narrow-minded common people and commit suicide by secretly jumping into an abyss."

18 The chief of staff, Xian, working for Gong Shu Wen Zi was recommended by Wen Zi to the duke of Wey (衛國). Both Gong Shu Wen Zi and Xian were promoted to prominent positions of the same rank. Confucius said, after hearing this news, "Gong Shu Wen Zi deserves to be called a Wen Zi indeed."

18a Gong Shu Wen Zi (公叔文子) was a minister of the state of Wey (衛國).

Xian (僎) was a manager of household affairs for Gong Shu Wen Zi.

The title of "Wen Zi" means a great and respectable scholar.

19 Confucius commented on Wey Ling Gong's incompetent and unprincipled governance style. Kang Zi said, "If so, why he is not yet toppled?" Confucius said, "He has Zhong Shu Yu in charge of diplomatic relations, Chu Tuo in charge of the management of ancestral temples, and Wang Sun Jia in charge of the army. Because of their competence, how can he be toppled?"

19a Wey Ling Gong (衛靈公) was the duke of Wey (衛國). Confucius once worked for him, was disgruntled, and left after nine months.

Ji Kang Zi (季康子, died 468 BC) was the prime minister of the state of Lu (魯國) during the reign of Ai Gong (哀公) and was the most powerful official.

Zhong Shu Yu (仲叔圉) was the minister for foreign affairs of the state of Wey (衛國).

Chu Tuo (祝鮀) was the minister for ceremonial affairs.

Wang Sun Jia (王孫賈) was the chief commander of the army.

20 Confucius said, "If one boasts recklessly, it will be difficult for him to keep his words."

21 Chen Cheng Zi assassinated Duke Jian of Qi (齊國). Confucius took a bath, went to the Imperial Court, and advised Ai Gong of the state of Lu, saying, "Chen Cheng assassinated his king. Please send an army to punish him." Ai Gong said, "You need to report to and consult the three prime ministers: Ji Sun, Su Sun, and Meng Sun." Confucius said, "Since I have been your minister, I must report to my king, but he said, 'Report and consult the three prime ministers.'" Confucius then went to see the three ministers, and they did not agree to invade Chen Cheng. Confucius said, "Since I have been a minister, it is my responsibility to report to them."

21a Chen Cheng Zi (陈成子) was a minister of the state of Qi (齊國). He assassinated Duke Jian of Qi (齊國) and supported the duke's younger brother, Qi Ping Gong (齊平公), to be the successor to Duke Jian and a puppet to Chen.

Ai Gong (哀公) was the duke of Lu (魯國) from 494 to 468 BC. He was dominated by the three prime ministers.

The three dominant families of the state of Lu (魯國) were the descendants of Meng Sun Si (孟孫 氏), Su Sun Si (叔孫氏), and Ji Sun Si (季孫氏). They are all prime ministers of the state.

22 Zi Lu asked how to best serve the king. Confucius said, "Do not cheat him. Advise him sincerely."

23 Confucius said, "A Jun Zi aims at high moral and virtuous grounds. A Xiao Ren aims at decadence."

24 Confucius said, "In ancient times, scholars learned with a view of self-improvement. Nowadays, scholars learn with a view of appraisal by people."

25 Qu Bo Yu sent a messenger to visit Confucius. Confucius sat down with the messenger and asked, "How does my friend Qu do?" The messenger replied, "My master tries relentlessly to reduce his own flaws and correct his past mistakes but has not yet succeeded." After the messenger left, Confucius exclaimed, "A good messenger indeed! A good messenger indeed!"

25a Qu Bo Yu (蘧伯玉, 585–484 BC) was a good friend of Confucius and a minister of the state of Wey (衛國). Qu was highly regarded by Confucius to be a virtuous person. Confucius once stayed at his home during Confucius's grand tour around many countries.

26 Confucius said, "If you do not have one particular official position, you do not work on [formulate] its policy." Zheng Zi added, "A Jun Zi worries about exceeding one's position."

Or:

Confucius said, "If the time and circumstance are not right, do not put forward an inappropriate policy." Zheng Zi added, "A Jun Zi worries about being untimely and out of place."

26a Zheng Zi (曾子, also known as Zheng Shen 曾參, born 505 BC) was a prominent disciple of Confucius, known for his filial piety. He was the author of *The Book of Great Learning* (大學).

This paragraph has been interpreted by many scholars in many ways. The above are two of them (see paragraph 14 of chapter 8).

The word *position* (位) may be interpreted as an official position in the government or as a point in time and space.

27 Confucius said, "A Jun Zi feels ashamed for boasting beyond his (intended future or past) actions."

28 Confucius said, "A Jun Zi maintains three moral mindsets, but I am unable to. A Ren person has no worries, a wise person has no delusions, and a brave person has no fears." Zi Gong said, "Master, you are describing yourself!"

28a Zi Gong (子貢, also known as Duan Mu Ci端木賜, born around 520 BC) was one of the top ten disciples of Confucius. He later became the prime minister of the states of Lu (魯國) and Wey (衛國). He also made a fortune in business and was the wealthiest disciple of Confucius. He advocated making money through propriety, honesty, and trust. His eloquence was also well known. After Confucius's death, Zi Gong observed six years of mourning vigil to show his deep respect for Confucius.

29 Zi Gong criticized and defamed someone. Confucius said, "Ci, are you faultless also? I don't have time to criticize and defame others."

29a Ci (賜) was the first name of Zi Gong.

30 Confucius said, "I am not concerned with not being known by others. I am concerned with my lack of ability."

31 Confucius said, "If one does not anticipate deception on him or loss of trust by others, yet can predict the reality beforehand, he is a virtuous person indeed!"

32 Wei Sheng Mu spoke to Confucius, "Why are you busy doing road shows all over the place? Do you want to show off your eloquence?" Confucius said, "I dare not show off my eloquence. I just hate stubborn blockheads."

32a Wei Sheng Mu (微生畝) was a hermit and a sage.

33 Confucius said, "A horse is regarded a thoroughbred not because of its strength but rather its superior characters."

34 Someone asked, "How about returning trespass against us with kindness? Is that really good?" Confucius replied, "With what will we return kindness to us then? We should deal with trespass against us with propriety, justice, and uprightness and return kindness to us with kindness."

34a This paragraph is important. Most scholars and common Chinese took the first sentence out of context and misunderstood that we should return trespass against us with kindness, like what other religions teach. Instead, Confucius questioned the logic of the first sentence. If we return kindness for both trespasses against us and kindness to us, we do not differentiate trespasses versus kindness in the first place. This approach is impractical in this world and will lead to uncontrollable chaos since unchecked evil will prevail. According to Confucius, the correct approach is to deal with evil with uprightness and justice. Confucius is more pragmatic and worldly than many other religious leaders and philosophers.

35 Confucius said, "Nobody understands me!" Zi Gong asked, "Why do you say that?" Confucius said, "I do not complain to heaven. I do not blame other people. I try to learn ordinary matters in the world and to reach highest morality standards. Only heaven understands me."

35a Zi Gong (子貢, also known as Duan Mu Ci端木賜, born around 520 BC) was one of the top ten disciples of Confucius. He later became the prime minister of the states of Lu (魯國) and Wey (衛國). He also made a fortune in business and was the wealthiest disciple of Confucius. He advocated making money through propriety, honesty, and trust. His eloquence was also well known. After Confucius's death, Zi Gong observed six years of mourning vigil to show his deep respect for Confucius.

36 Gong Bo Liao slandered Zi Lu to Ji Sun Si. Zi Fu Jing Bo heard about it and told Confucius, saying, "Ji Sun Si was misled by Gong Bo Liao. I have the power to slaughter Gong Bo Liao and expose his corpse in the public square." Confucius said, "Will universal laws of nature and morality prevail? Well, it is fate. Will universal laws of nature and morality be abolished? It is also fate. Can Gong Bo Liao change fate?"

36a Gong Bo Liao (公伯寮) was a disciple of Confucius and a colleague of Zi Lu (子路), working for Ji Sun, a powerful minister of the state of Lu (魯國).

Ji Ping Zi (季平子, also known as Ji Sun Si季孫氏, died 505 BC) was a descendant of a powerful family of the state of Lu (魯國) and its prime minister.

Zi Lu (子路, 542–480 BC also known as Zhong You, 仲由) was best known for his ability and success in statesmanship. He was noted for his valor and sense of justice.

Zi Fu Jing Bo (子服景伯) was a senior minister of the state of Lu (魯國). Zi Fu was his family name, and Jing Bo was his first name.

37 Confucius said, "Persons with superior virtue would escape from a decadent world and become hermits. If that is not feasible,

they would emigrate to another place. If that is not feasible, they would avoid meeting ugly people. If that is not feasible still, they would avoid talking." Confucius said, "Only seven persons I know of can do so."

37a The seven persons were Bo Yi (伯夷), Shu Qi (叔齊), Yu Zhong (虞仲, also known as Zhong Yong, 仲雍), Yi Yi (夷逸), Zhu Zhang (朱張), Liu Xia Hui (柳下惠), and Lu Shao Lian (魯少連).

Bo Yi (伯夷) and Shu Qi (叔齊) were two princes of the last duke of the feudal state of Gu Zhu (孤竹國), during the Shang Dynasty (商朝, 1766–1046 BC). Bo Yi was the eldest brother, and Shu Qi was the youngest. Before their father died, Shu Qi was nominated to be his successor. Shu Qi abdicated his throne to his eldest brother, Bo Yi, and stressed that the eldest son should be the successor to the throne according to tradition. Bo Yi refused to accept because of the respect of his father's wish. Both eventually renounced the throne and migrated to the territory of the state of Zhou (周). Later, King Wu of Zhou (周武王) raised an army to invade the Shang Dynasty. Both Bo Yi and Shu Qi knelt in front of King Wu's chariot and begged King Wu not to invade the Shang Dynasty. King Wu eventually conquered the Shang Dynasty and founded the Zhou Dynasty (周朝). Bo Yi and Shu Qi refused to be subjects of the Zhou Dynasty and eat its food. They moved to the mountains and starved to death. These two ancient characters were regarded by historians to be model Jun Zis who had the Ren virtue.

King Tai (周太王) of the state of Zhou had three sons: Tai Bo (泰伯), Zhong Yong (仲雍), and Ji Li (季歷). The youngest son, Ji Li, had a son, Chong (昌), who was regarded the best candidate to be the future leader of the country. Tai Bo left the country with his younger brother Zhong Yong to give way to Ji Li. Because of this, King Tai designated Ji Li to be his successor so that Chong would eventually become the king of the country. Tai Bo cut his hair and put on tattoos so that people could not recognize his identity. Later, Ji Li became the King Wen of Zhou (周文王), and after his death, Chong became King Wu of Zhou (周武王), who founded the Zhou Dynasty (周朝). King Wen was regarded by Confucius and other historians as a saintly king.

Tai Bo abdicated the throne three times. The first time, Tai Bo left the country quietly when he was aware that his father liked the grandson Chong very much. The second time, Tai Bo returned to attend his father's funeral, and Ji Li offered him the throne, but Tai Bo still rejected the offer. The third time, when Ji Li was killed in a battle, ministers in court supported Tai Bo to take the throne. Tai Bo still abdicated the throne to Chong, knowing that Chong would become a better leader.

Confucius praised Tai Bo and Yu Zhong for their concession of the throne.

Little was known about Yi Yi, and he was believed be a hermit. He once told people that he would rather be a cow toiling in the field than an official in a corrupt government.

Zhu Zhang was another ancient hermit. Little was known about him.

Liu Xia Hui (柳下惠, 720–621 BC) was once an official of the state of Lu (魯國). He later resigned and became a hermit. He was fired three times as the chief justice. Somebody asked him why he did not find a job in another country. He replied, "Since I act properly all the time, which country would not fire me?" (see chapter 18, paragraph 2 and 8).

There was also a famous episode about him. It was freezing, snowy evening when he was traveling. He went into a ruined temple for shelter. Soon afterward, a beautiful woman came in. She shivered and begged to sit on his lap and embrace each other to keep warm. He refused at first, claiming that it was inappropriate. She insisted and said that if she died, nobody would take care of her elderly mother. He finally agreed, held the woman on his lap, and shared his coat with her. During the entire evening, while she was being warmed, he did not harass her sexually. He was later praised by historians for being able to resist sexual temptation even with a beauty sitting on his lap.

Little was known about Lu Shao Lian.

38 Zi Lu stayed overnight in the suburb of the capital of the state of Lu (魯國). He entered the city early the next morning. The guard at the city gate questioned him, "Where do you come from?" Zi Lu replied, "From Confucius's school." That guard said, "Ah, that man who insists on doing things that he knows are infeasible."

38a Zi Lu (子路, 542–480 BC), also called Zhong You (仲由), was a disciple of Confucius and was best known for his ability and success in statesmanship. He was also noted for his valor and sense of justice.

39 Confucius played a piece of percussion music on a drum made of stone. A stranger carrying a straw basket passed by Confucius's house. He exclaimed, "The player of this music is upset!" He further said, "It sounds like narrow-minded obstinacy. When nobody appreciates you, mind your own business instead. When you are in deep water, swim with your clothes on. When you are in shallow water, roll up your trousers and walk across." Confucius said, "Too critical indeed. I cannot change his view."

39a That person could tell from Confucius's performance that Confucius was frustrated because nobody took his philosophy seriously. The key sentences were taken from *The Book of Poetry*. "When you are in deep water, swim with your clothes on." "When you are in shallow water, roll up your trousers and walk across." These verses meant that one should be pragmatic and adapt to the prevailing circumstance. Do not be stubborn.

41 Zi Zhang said, "*The Book of History* mentioned that Gao Zhong did not talk for three years during the mourning vigil in remembrance of his father." Confucius said, "Why do you single out Gao Zhong as an example? All ancient people did the same. When the king died, all his ministers must observe for three years the rules dictated by the prime minister."

41a Zi Zhang (子張, 503–447 BC) was a disciple of Confucius.

Gao Zhong (高宗) was an emperor in the Shang Dynasty (商朝).

42 Confucius said, "If the leader cherishes Li, his people can be governed easily."

42a The word *Li* (禮) in Confucianism and in the Chinese language in general has many meanings. In ancient times, it referred to rites, rituals in ceremonies, protocols in courts and government, discipline, regulations, laws and order, respect, courtesy, and etiquette in daily life; in modern times, it refers to respect, etiquette, courtesy, presents, and gifts. Li (禮) includes a set of social norms that are motivated by the inner conscience of people and entrenched in the culture rather than externally imposed by the government through decrees and legislation (see endnote 7).

43 Zi Lu asked what constitutes a Jun Zi. Confucius said, "Cultivate yourself so that you can take your responsibilities seriously and respectfully." Zi Lu asked, "Is that all?" Confucius said, "Cultivate yourself so that you can bring peace and happiness

to your family and fellow men." Zi Lu further asked, "Is that all?" Confucius said, "Cultivate yourself so that you can bring peace and happiness to all people in the world. Even Yao and Shun would find it difficult to accomplish this ideal."

43a Yao (堯, 2356–2255 BC) and Shun (舜, 2294–2184 BC) were the two saintly kings who founded a utopian society in ancient China.

44 Yuan Ran squatted impolitely with his legs wide open while he was waiting for Confucius, who then reprimanded Yuan, "If you are not modest and polite while young, you will do nothing worthy when you grow up, and you will idle away till death. This is reprimandable." Confucius then hit Yuan's leg with a staff.

44a Yuan Ran (原壤) was a disciple of Confucius.

45 Confucius hired a youth from his own village Qufu to be a messenger. Someone asked Confucius, "Does he have a promising future?" Confucius said, "I often saw him sitting on seats reserved for adults and walking shoulder to shoulder with seniors. He is not sincerely interested in self-improvement. He is just anxious to become a grown-up."

45a The village Qufu was Confucius's hometown.

CHAPTER 15

WEY LING GONG (衛靈公)

1 Wey Ling Gong asked Confucius about military tactics. Confucius replied, "I have heard of ceremonial rituals for the worship of ancestors. I have not learned military affairs." Confucius left the next day.

1a Wey Ling Gong (衛靈公, 540–493 BC) was the duke of Wey (衛國). Confucius once worked for him for nine months (see paragraph 13a of chapter 3, paragraph 28a of chapter 6, and paragraph 18a of chapter 9).

2 Confucius was stuck in the state of Chen, and his food and provisions were exhausted. His followers were so hungry and sick that they could not get up. The worried and frustrated Zi Lu complained to Confucius, "Why does a Jun Zi also need to suffer poverty?" Confucius said, "A Jun Zi endures poverty firmly. A Xiao Ren commits plunders when he is poor."

2a Zi Lu (子路, 542–480 BC), also called Zhong You (仲由), was a disciple of Confucius and was best known for his ability and success in statesmanship. He was also noted for his valor and sense of justice.

3 Confucius asked Zi Gong, "Ci, do you think that I am a knowledgeable and learned person?" Li Gong said, "Yes, are you not?" Confucius said, "No, I am just persistent only."

3a Zi Gong (子貢, also known as Duan Mu Ci端木賜, born around 520 BC) was one of the top ten disciples of Confucius. He later became the prime minister of the states of Lu (魯國) and Wey (衛國). He also made a fortune in business and was the wealthiest disciple of Confucius. He advocated making money through propriety, honesty, and trust. His eloquence was also well known. After Confucius's death, Zi Gong observed six years of mourning vigil to show his deep respect for Confucius.

4 Confucius spoke to Zi Lu, "Zhong You, very few people know moral and virtuous principles."

4a Zi Lu (子路, 542–480 BC), also called Zhong You (仲由), was a disciple of Confucius and was best known for his ability and success in statesmanship. He was also noted for his valor and sense of justice.

5 Confucius said, "There was only one ruler in history who could govern the country well and bring peace and prosperity to it without artificial and deliberate interventions and interference. This was Shun. How did he do so? He conducted himself properly and seriously respected his role as a ruler and set an example, so he could sit on his throne comfortably by delegation to ministers who emulated him."

5a The phrase "to govern the country well and bring peace and prosperity to it without artificial and deliberate interventions and interference" (無為而治) was the same concept advocated by Lao Tze (老子, also known as Laozi, 571–471 BC), the founder of Taoism.

Shun (舜, 2294–2184 BC) was a successor of Yao (堯, 2356–2255 BC). These two emperors are regarded by historians as saints.

6 Zi Zhang asked about the proper conduct for a man. Confucius said, "If one is honest and trustworthy in his words, and serious and respectful in his actions, he can function even in a barbaric country. If not, he cannot function even inside his own village. When he stands up, he should visualize such mottos as if they are shown before his eyes. When he sits in a carriage, he should visualize such mottos as if they are engraved on a wooden plank in front of him." Zi Zhang then wrote these words on his belt.

6a Zi Zhang (子張, 503–447 BC) was a disciple of Confucius.

7 Confucius said, "Shi Yu was upright indeed! When the government was good, he acted like an arrow. When it was bad, he also acted like an arrow. Qu Bo Yu was a Jun Zi indeed! When the government was good, he joined as a minister. When the government was bad, he quit."

7a Shi Yu (史魚, also known as Zi Yu, 子魚) was a minister of the state of Wey in charge of ceremonial affairs. He recommended Qu Bo Yu to Wey Ling Gong (衛靈公), the duke of Wey (衛國).

Qu Bo Yu (蘧伯玉, 585–484 BC) was a good friend of Confucius and a minister of the state of Wey (衛國). Qu was highly regarded by Confucius to be a virtuous person. Confucius once stayed at his home during Confucius's grand tour to many countries.

8 Confucius said, "When it is appropriate and feasible to speak [and give advice] to a person, but you refrain from doing so, you will lose a friend. When it is inappropriate or infeasible to speak to a person, but you speak anyhow, you misspeak."

9 Confucius said, "A hero who is determined to uphold the Ren virtue would not seek to live at the expense of hurting his Ren virtue, but he would sacrifice his life in order to preserve it."

10 Zi Gong asked about Ren virtue. Confucius said, "When a craftsman [technician] wants to do a good job, he must sharpen his tools beforehand. After you have arrived in that country [and reported to work], serve and align yourself with competent and virtuous officials working for the prime minister and befriend colleagues who have the Ren virtue."

10a Zi Gong (子貢, also known as Duan Mu Ci端木賜, born around 520 BC) was one of the top ten disciples of Confucius. He later became the prime minister of the states of Lu (魯國) and Wey (衛國). He also made a fortune in business and was the wealthiest disciple of Confucius. He advocated making money through propriety, honesty, and trust. His eloquence was also well known. After Confucius's death, Zi Gong observed six years of mourning vigil to show his deep respect for Confucius.

Confucius reminded Zi Gong of the above principle when he first became an official of the state of Wey (衛國).

11 Yan Yuan asked how to govern a country. Confucius said, "Follow the calendar and almanac of the Xia Dynasty, ride on carriages of the Yin Dynasty, wear the hats of the Zhou Dynasty, and play music of Shao with its pantomimes. Banish the music of the state of Zheng and stay away from crooked and fawning people. The

music [and pantomimes] of Zheng is kinky [and obscene]. Crooked and fawning people are dangerous."

11a Yan Hui (颜回, also known as Yan Yuan顏淵, 521–481 BC) was the best disciple of Confucius. Confucius held him in the highest regard among his disciples.

The Xia Dynasty (夏朝) was from about 2070 to 1766 BC. The Yan Dynasty (殷朝) was also called the Shang Dynasty (商朝) and was from about 1766 to 1046 BC. The Zhou Dynasty (周朝) was from about 1046 to 256 BC.

The music of Shao (韶) was believed to be composed by Emperor Shun (舜, 2294–2184 BC) or during his reign. It was regarded as sacred classical music during Confucius's era.

The music of Zheng (鄭聲) was regarded as pop music during Confucius's era.

12 Confucius said, "If a person does not plan and prepare for the future, he must be beset by worries and troubles very soon."

13 Confucius lamented, "It is all over! I have never seen anyone who loves virtues as much as sexy women."

13a This paragraph is the same as paragraph 18 of chapter 9.

14 Confucius said, "Zang Wen Zhong abused his position and power. Although he knew that Liu Xia Hui was competent and virtuous, Zang still did not appoint Liu to a position."

14a Zang Wen Zhong (臧文仲, died 617 BC) was a statesman of the state of Qi (齊國) before Confucius.

Liu Xia Hui (柳下惠, 720–621 BC) was once an official of the state of Lu (魯國). He later resigned and became a hermit. He was fired three times as the chief justice. Somebody asked him why he did not find a job in another country. He replied, "Since I act properly all the time, which country would not fire me?"

15 Confucius said, "If you set a high standard for yourself and a lower one for others, you will avoid resentment."

16 Confucius said, "I do not know how to deal with those people who never ask, 'How do I do this? How do I do that?'"

17 Confucius said, "Those who gather with friends, gossip all day, and show off their trivial shrewdness have difficulty making serious progress in life."

18 Confucius said, "A Jun Zi regards righteousness and honor as fundamental bases, acts in line with Li, shows humility, delivers promises, and completes contracts with sincerity and trust. If so, he is indeed a Jun Zi."

18a Li (禮) in Confucianism and in the Chinese language in general has many meanings. In ancient times, it referred to rites, rituals in ceremonies, protocols in courts and government, discipline, regulations, laws and order, respect, courtesy, and etiquette in daily life; in modern times, it refers to respect, etiquette, courtesy, presents, and gifts. In the context of this paragraph, this word has the ancient meaning (see endnote 7).

19 Confucius said, "A Jun Zi is disappointed about his own incompetency. He is not distressed that he is not known by others."

20 Confucius said, "A Jun Zi dreads that no one will mention his name after his death."

21 Confucius said, "A Jun Zi expects a lot of himself. A Xiao Ren expects a lot from others."

Or:

Confucius said, "A Jun Zi sets a high standard for himself. A Xiao Ren sets a high standard for others."

Or:

Confucius said, "A Jun Zi depends on himself to do good. A Xiao Ren relies on others to do good."

22 Confucius said, "A Jun Zi is respectful and dignified. He is a team player but not a partisan."

23 Confucius said, "A Jun Zi does not appoint and promote a person because of his words only and does not categorically ignore or censor a person's words no matter who he is."

24 Zi Gong asked Confucius, "Is there a motto for me to remember for life?" Confucius said, "Is this not forgiveness and reciprocity? Don't do onto others what you don't want."

24a This is a common sentence in Chinese and other cultures.

25 Confucius said, "When I evaluate who deserves blame and who deserves praise, I examine his actual deeds before I attribute praise or blame. In this regard, the well-being of all people nowadays is due to righteous and benevolent policies of the Xia, Shang, and Zhou Dynasties."

25a The Xia Dynasty (夏朝) was from about 2070 to 1766 BC. The Yan Dynasty (殷朝) was also called the Shang Dynasty (商朝)

and was from about 1766 to 1046 BC. The Zhou Dynasty (周朝) was from about 1046 to 256 BC.

26 Confucius said, "Even in my early days, historians would omit recording an episode that could not be verified and validated. Horse owners would lend their horses to others for free rides. Alas, there are no such things now."

27 Confucius said, "Flowery words confound virtue. Slight lack of patience and forbearance ruin a great strategy."

28 Confucius said, "When the multitudes hate a person or phenomenon, it is necessary to carefully examine the validity of the case. When the multitudes love a person or phenomenon, it is also necessary to carefully examine the validity of the case."

28a This paragraph says that we should critically think and avoid herd behavior.

29 Confucius said, "Man can promote moral principles and standards. Moral principles and standards should not be used to promote man."

29a The second sentence hints against hypocrisy. Some hypocrites promote their fame and status under the guise of moral principles and standards.

30 Confucius said, "Not correcting one's fault is a real fault indeed."

31 Confucius said, "I have tried to ponder day and night without eating and sleep. It was useless. It is better to learn."

32 Confucius said, "The primary focus of a Jun Zi is in the cultivation of virtue and attainment of high moral standards and not food. Farmers sometimes need to suffer from famines. Serious

scholars can be rewarded with emoluments. A Jun Zi is concerned with his lack of moral standards—not of poverty."

33 Confucius said, "If one becomes an official by his knowledge and academic qualifications but does not maintain such qualities according to Ren principles, he may not be able to keep his position for long. If he becomes an official by his knowledge and academic qualifications, maintains such qualities according to Ren principles, but does not take his responsibilities seriously, his people will not respect him. If he becomes an official by his knowledge and academic qualifications, maintains such qualities according to Ren principles, takes his responsibilities seriously, but acts against Li principles, he is still not faultless."

33a Ren (仁) embodies all virtues of humanity, including love (see endnote 3).

The word *Li* (禮) in Confucianism and in the Chinese language in general has many meanings. In ancient times, it referred to rites, rituals in ceremonies, protocols in courts and government, discipline, regulations, laws and order, respect, courtesy, and etiquette in daily life; in modern times, it refers to respect, etiquette, courtesy, presents, and gifts. Li (禮) includes a set of social norms that are motivated by the inner conscience of people and entrenched in the culture rather than externally imposed by the government through decrees and legislation (see endnote 7).

34 Confucius said, "A Jun Zi is not known for trivial matters but can be entrusted with major responsibilities and challenges. A Xiao Ren cannot be entrusted with major responsibilities and challenges but is known for trivial matters."

35 Confucius said, "Ren virtue is more to man than water and fire. I have seen men die from treading water and fire, but I have never seen a man die from following Ren virtue."

37 Confucius said, "When confronted with a challenge of upholding Ren virtue or not, one should not yield—not even to his own teacher."

38 Confucius said, "A Jun Zi should firmly stick to righteousness and disregard mean promises."

38a Mean promises refer to promises to friends who ask for small favors due to friendship.

39 Confucius said, "The proper way to serve your king [boss] is to take your responsibilities seriously and perform before asking for a salary and bonus."

40 Confucius said, "I teach everybody irrespective of their background, class, and type."

41 Confucius said, "When our goal and path are different, we do not plot together."

42 Confucius said, "The sole purpose of a language is to communicate messages and ideas. That is all."

43 The music master, Mian, visited Confucius. When the master came to the doorstep, Confucius said, "Here are the steps." When the master came to the mat, Confucius said, "Here is the mat." After all were seated, Confucius said, "So-and-so is here, and so-and-so is also here." After the master left, Zi Zhang asked, "Why did you tell those trivial things to the master?" Confucius said, "Of course, this is the way to lead the blind."

43a Zi Zhang (子張, 503–447 BC) was a disciple of Confucius.

CHAPTER 16

JI SI (季氏)

1 Ji Si planned to invade a small country, Zhuan Yu. Ran You and Ji Lu consulted Confucius, "Ji Si is about to invade Zhuan Yu." Confucius said, "Qiu, is it not your fault? Our former king appointed the ruler of Zhuan Yu to preside over the worship of the east mountain Mang. This country has since become a colony of the state of Lu. Its ruler is therefore a subject of our king. Why should it be invaded?" Ran You replied, "Our boss wants to do so. We both disagree with the invasion." Confucius said, "Qiu, Zhou Ren once said that when your sincere advice is listened to by your boss, you stay, and if not, you quit. If you do not support your boss when he is in danger, or you do not lift him up when he falls, why should your boss hire you? What you just said is wrong. When a tiger or female rhinoceros escapes from the cage, or a sacred tortoise shell or a piece of jade is injured or damaged in the royal repository, whose fault is it?" Ran You defended, "But Zhuan Yu is strong and located near the city of Fei. If we do not subdue it now, it will become a serious threat to our descendants." Confucius said, "A Jun Zi hates to give excuses to justify his greed. I have heard that rulers of countries and provinces are not troubled by the small size of the population of their states but are troubled by the inequality among their people. They are not troubled by poverty but are troubled by national instability

and insecurity. If there is equality, there will be no poverty and no scarcity of population. If there is peace in society, there will be no revolt. Therefore, if a foreign country does not want to join your union, you attract it with your high standard of civilization and morality. Once it has joined your country, they must be made content and settled. My Ran You and Qi, since you are good advisors to your boss, Ji Si, you should understand that if a foreign country is not impressed, it will not join you. When the country is divisive, you cannot prevent it from disintegration by simply waging a war against your own constituents. I am worried for Ji Si, not so much for Zhuan Yu, because the disaster is looming inside the imperial court."

1a Ji Si (季氏) was one of the three dominant families of the state of Lu (魯國), Confucius's motherland.

Zi You (子有, also known as Ran You, 冉有, Ran Qiu, 冉求 born in 522 BC) was the chief of staff of the Ji Si family and a disciple of Confucius.

Zi Lu (子路, 542–480 BC was also called Zhong You, 仲由, Ji Lu, 季路). Among Confucius's disciples, he was best known for his ability and success in statesmanship.

Zhuan Yu (顓臾) was a small country and a colony of the state of Lu (魯國).

Zhou Ren (周任) was a famous historian in the Zhou Dynasty (周朝, around 1043–256 BC).

This conversation highlighted Confucius's political philosophy. The key words here are *equality, stability, security, no poverty, high standard of civilization and morality,* and *unity.*

2 Confucius said, "When a good government prevails in the empire, the establishment of ceremonial, musical standards, norms, and the waging of wars should come from the imperial emperor. When a bad government prevails, such powers are in the hands of princes and lords. When they control the power to rule the empire, they seldom stay in power for more than ten generations. When ministers control the power to rule the empire, they seldom stay in power for more than five generations. When lower-level ministers control the power to rule the empire, they seldom stay in power for more than three generations. When a good government prevails, the power to rule the empire should not be in the hands of ministers. When a good government prevails, common people will not protest."

3 Confucius said, "The royal family of the state of Lu has lost the power to rule the country for five generations. The government has been controlled by ministers for another four generations. Nowadays, the country, ruled by three descendants of Duke Huan, is declining."

3a The three dominant families of the state of Lu (魯國) were the descendants of Meng Sun Si (孟孫氏), Su Sun Si (叔孫氏), and Ji Sun Si (季孫氏). They dominated the court of the state of Lu. They were all descendants of Duke Huan (魯桓公).

4 Confucius said, "There are three types of beneficial friends and three types of harmful friends. Upright friends, trustworthy friends, and knowledgeable friends are beneficial. Friends who flatter, slander you behind your back, or talk in flowery words are harmful."

5 Confucius said, "There are three types of beneficial enjoyment and three types of harmful enjoyment. Enjoyment in classical music, rituals, and pantomimes, enjoyment in helping others, and enjoyment in making virtuous friends are beneficial. Enjoyment in a

lavish and decadent lifestyle, enjoyment in loitering, and enjoyment in partying and feasting are harmful."

6 Confucius said, "One can make three types of mistakes when talking to a Jun Zi [and a superior]. Speaking out before his turn to speak is rashness. Not speaking when it is his turn to speak is concealment. Ignoring the facial gestures and body language of the Jun Zi [and a superior] is called blindness."

7 Confucius said, "A Jun Zi has three abstinences: when he is young, energetic, and desirous, he needs to abstain from lust; when he is a strong grown-up, he needs to abstain from fighting with people; when he is old, he needs to abstain from greed."

8 Confucius said, "A Jun Zi is in awe of three things: he is in awe of divine providence, in awe of great men, and in awe of words of sages. A Xiao Ren does not know divine providence and therefore is not in awe of it. He abuses great men and refutes the words of sages."

9 Confucius said, "Those who are born with knowledge and wisdom are at the top. Those who acquire knowledge through learning are next. Those who learn when in need are further below. Those who do not learn when in need are at the bottom."

10 Confucius said, "A Jun Zi has nine types of thoughtful considerations: When he sees, can he see clearly? When he hears, can he hear clearly? Is his countenance mild? Is his demeanor respectful? Are his words sincere? Is he devoted to his work? Does he ask questions when he is in doubt? When he acts in anger, does he consider the negative consequences? When he sees a profit or gain, does he think of righteousness?"

11 Confucius said, "Some people hurry up to catch an opportunity to do good and stay away from evil as if he would

avoid dipping his hand into boiling water. I have seen such people and heard their words. Some people become hermits to uphold their noble principles and practice righteousness to follow their way to morality. I have heard their words, but I have not seen them."

12 Qi Jing Gong had thousands of horses. When he died, his people did not praise him for his virtue. Bo Yi and Shu Qi starved to death in the mountains of Shou Yang. People have since praised them as saints. This illustrates what matters.

12a Qi Jing Gong (齊景公) was the duke of Qi (齊國). According to historians, he was not a good king. He indulged in lavishness, pleasure, and lust, and he did not care about the welfare of his people.

Bo Yi (伯夷) and Shu Qi (叔齊) were two princes of the last duke of the feudal state of Gu Zhu (孤竹國), during the Shang Dynasty (商朝, 1766–1046 BC). Bo Yi was the eldest brother and Shu Qi was the youngest. Before their father died, Shu Qi was nominated to be his successor. Shu Qi abdicated his throne to his eldest brother, Bo Yi, and stressed that the eldest son should be the successor to the throne according to tradition. Bo Yi refused to accept because of the respect of his father's wish. Both eventually renounced the throne and migrated to the territory of the state of Zhou (周). Later, King Wu of Zhou (周武王) raised an army to invade the Shang Dynasty. Both Bo Yi and Shu Qi knelt in front of King Wu's chariot and begged King Wu not to invade the Shang Dynasty. King Wu eventually conquered the Shang Dynasty and founded the Zhou Dynasty (周朝). Bo Yi and Shu Qi refused to be subjects of the Zhou Dynasty and eat its food. They moved to the mountains and starved to death. These two ancient characters were regarded by historians to be model Jun Zis who had the Ren virtue.

13 Chen Kang asked Bo Yu, "Have you learned any lesson from your father different from what we have learned?" Bo Yu replied, "No. I once passed by him when he was standing alone in the hall. He asked me, 'Have you studied *The Book of Poetry* yet?' I said: 'No.' He then told me, 'If you don't know the odes, you are not fit to talk to.' I then retreated and studied *The Book of Poetry*. On another day, I also passed by him hastily. He asked me, 'Have you studied the rules under Li?' I replied, 'No.' He then told me, 'If you don't know Li, you cannot establish yourself.' I then retreated and learned Li. I have only heard these two pieces of advice from him." Chen Kang left and was impressed, saying, "I have heard three things: it is important to study *The Book of Poetry* and to learn Li. I also learned that a Jun Zi should not pamper his son."

13a Chen Kang (陳亢) was a disciple of Confucius.

Bo Yu (伯魚, also known as Li, 鯉) was the son of Confucius.

14 The king called his wife "My Lady." She called herself "Little Girl." The people of his kingdom called her "Your Majesty Lady." Foreigners called her "Your Majesty Little Lady." They also called her "Your Majesty Lady."

CHAPTER 17

YANG HUO (陽貨)

1 Yang Huo wanted to see Confucius, but Confucius refused to see him. Yang Huo then sent a roast pig to Confucius as a friendly gesture. Confucius then went to see him while he was out. They later met on the road. Yang Huo said to Confucius, "Come, I need to talk to you." He then said, "If one possesses an outstanding caliber like a precious jewel but stands aloof from chaos in the country, can he be regarded to have Ren virtue?" Confucius said, "No, he cannot." Yang Huo then said, "If one is interested in public services but misses great opportunities, is he wise?" Confucius said, "No, he is not." Yang Huo then said, "Time flies. It does not wait for us." Confucius said, "Yes. I will look for an official job then."

1a Yang Huo (陽貨, also known as Yang Hu 陽虎) was the top official working for the Ji Si family. Confucius despised him and regarded him as a malicious official. Yang Huo wanted to recruit Confucius to work for him, but Confucius had turned down his offer before. Since Yang Huo sent him a gift, Confucius needed to pay him a visit to thank him according to normal etiquette.

2 Confucius said, "The inborn nature of everybody is similar. Environmental influences, habits, education, and culture set people apart."

2a This is a fundamental philosophical doctrine of Confucianism, Taoism, and Buddhism.

3 Confucius said, "Only superior wisdom and extreme stupidity cannot be changed."

4 Confucius visited City Wu and heard lute and string music everywhere. Confucius was impressed, smiled, and said, "Why do you need to kill a kitchen with a big knife intended for slaughtering a cow?" Zi You defended, "Yan heard from you, Master, that after a Jun Zi has learned virtuous principles, he will love his people, and after common people have learned virtuous principles, they can be governed easily." Confucius said, "My student, Yan, you are correct. Excuse me. I just spoke jokingly."

4a Zi You (子游, also known as Yan Yan, 言偃, 506–443 BC) was a prominent disciple of Confucius. At that time, he was the mayor of Wu in the state of Lu (魯國). It was a small city, but Zi You governed it as if it was a big country. He applied Confucius's teachings and promoted music and cultural activities to cultivate the citizens of the city.

"Killing a chicken with a big knife intended for slaughtering a cow" is a common Chinese proverb.

5 Gong Shan Fo Rao, the governor of the county of Fei, planned to start a rebellion against the government of the state of Lu. He invited Confucius to join him. Confucius wanted to go. Zi Lu was upset about Confucius and said, "Do you have nowhere to go? Why do you need to join Gong Shan Fo Rao?" Confucius said, "He invited me not without a purpose. If I am hired, I will convert that county into a place like it used to be during the early Zhou Dynasty."

5a Gong Shan Fo Rao (公山弗擾) was a senior official working for the Ji Si family, who dominated the government of the state of Lu (魯國).

Zi Lu (子路, 542–480 BC also known as Zhong You 仲由) was best known for his ability and success in statesmanship. He was noted for his valor and sense of justice.

6 Zi Zhang asked what constituted Ren virtues. Confucius said, "If one can practice five virtues everywhere in the world, he can be regarded to have Ren virtues." Zi Zhang asked Confucius to elaborate. Confucius said, "Respect, generosity, sincerity, earnestness, and kindness. If you act respectfully, you will not be shamed. If you are generous, you will win the hearts of people. If you are sincere, people will trust you. If you are earnest, you can succeed. If you are kind, people will follow your orders."

6a Zi Zhang (子張, 503–447 BC) was a disciple of Confucius.

7 Fo Xi wanted to recruit Confucius, who was interested to join him. Zi Lu spoke to Confucius, "I remember that you once said, 'If a man does evil personally, a Jun Zi would not associate with him.' Fo Xi took possession of Zhong Mou and plots to rebel against the government. If you, Master, go to join him, what is your justification?" Confucius said, "Yes, I have said that before. A hard rock cannot be scraped thin. A pristine white cloth cannot be dyed black. Am I just a bottle gourd that is hung around a person's waist and cannot be eaten?"

7a A bottle gourd is also known as a calabash. It is a kind of melon and has the shape of a bottle. Ancient Chinese hollowed out its meat, dried its skin, and used the dried shell as a bottle.

8 Confucius said, "Zhong You, have you heard about six types of virtues and six flaws." Zhong You replied, "I have not." Confucius said, "Sit down. Let me tell you. The love of benevolence and kindness without the quest for learning would lead to the flaw of foolish simplicity. The love of knowledge without the quest for learning would lead to the flaw of aimless flirting. The love of sincerity without the quest for learning would lead to the flaw of being credulous. The love of being straightforward without the quest for learning would lead to the flaw of rudeness. The love of boldness without the quest for learning would lead to the flaw of violence. The love of firmness without the quest for learning would lead to the flaw of defiance."

8a Zi Lu (子路, 542–480 BC also known as Zhong You 仲由) was best known for his ability and success in statesmanship. He was noted for his valor and sense of justice.

9 Confucius said, "My students, why don't you study *The Book of Poetry*? Its poems can serve to express one's mind and emotions, can be read, can be recited among a group of friends, and can be used to communicate resentment. It can also be used to serve your parents at home and the king afar. You can also learn the names of birds, animals, trees, and plants from this book."

10 Confucius told his son Bo Yu, "Have you studied 'Zhou Nan' and 'Shao Nan' already? A man who has not studied 'Zhou Nan' and 'Shao Nan' is like someone who stands with his face pressed against a wall."

10a Bo Yu (伯魚, also known as Li, 鯉) was the son of Confucius.

"Zhou Nan (周南)" and "Shao Nan (召南)" are two chapters of the section of national folk songs (國風) in *The Book of Poetry* (詩經) (see endnotes 6 and 11).

11 Confucius said, "They say it is about Li rituals. They say it is about Li rituals. What is the point of showing off jade and silk in these rituals? They say it is about music. They say it is about music. What is the point of sounding bells and drums during musical performances?"

11a Confucius's point was that the essence of Li and music is in the spirit and not in material and superficial appearances.

12 Confucius said, "If one puts on a stern and firm appearance but is weak inside, is he like a petty burglar?"

13 Confucius said, "Following the herd without independent thinking of what is right or wrong would impair morality."

14 Confucius said, "Listening to hearsay will cast away morality."

15 Confucius said, "Those scumbags! How can we work with them to serve our king? When they have not got what they want, they are anxious to get it. After they have gotten it, they are anxious to keep it. They will do everything possible—including evil acts—to keep what they have gotten."

16 Confucius said, "Ancient people had three flaws, but they no longer prevail now. Bumptious people in the past did not care about trivial details, but bumptious people nowadays are unbridled; conservative people in the past were reserved, but conservative people nowadays are stubborn and abusive; stupid people in the past were straightforward, but stupid people nowadays are crooked."

17 Confucius said, "Flowery words and fawning manners seldom are Ren."

17a This sentence has also appeared in paragraph 3 of chapter 1.

18 Confucius said, "I hate the purple color taking away the luster of the red color. I hate the music of Zheng confounding the classical Ya music. I hate people who ruin their country with glib language."

18a The music of Zheng (鄭聲) was analogous to modern pop music, whereas the music of Ya (雅樂) was analogous to classical music.

19 Confucius said, "I do not want to talk anymore." Zi Gong said, "If you, Master, do not talk, how can we, your disciples, relate your teachings?" Confucius said, "What has nature said? The change of seasons, the regeneration of all living things. Are these what nature has taught us already?"

20 Ru Bei wanted to see Confucius, but Confucius declined with an excuse of being sick. After the messenger left the house, Confucius played the lute deliberately so that the messenger could hear the music.

20a Confucius considered that Ru Bei (孺悲) was not sincere in learning.

21 Zai Wo asked, "After our parents have died, we are supposed to observe mourning vigil for three years. It is too long. If a Jun Zi does not practice Li rituals for three years, the rituals will become slackened. If he does not play music for three years, his musical skills will be gone. Old grains will be exhausted and replaced by new grains. Firewood will need to be replenished. Therefore, one year of vigil should be enough." Confucius said, "Are you comfortable with that?" "If you feel comfortable, do it then! During a mourning period, a Jun Zi does not find food tasty, music enjoyable, and daily

life comfortable. Since you feel comfortable, you can do so for one year." Zai Wo left. Confucius then said, "He does not have Ren virtue. After a child is born, parents need to nurse the child for three years. Therefore, it is a common norm that children need to observe three years of mourning after the death of parents. Will Zai Wo give his parents three years of love?"

21a Zai Wo (宰我, also known as Zai Yu, 宰予, 522–458 BC) was among the top disciples of Confucius.

22 Confucius said, "If a person is well fed the whole day and does not use his brain on anything, it will be difficult for him to be of value in life. Are there poker games and chess? Playing these games is still more beneficial than doing nothing."

23 Zi Lu asked, "Should a Jun Zi esteem valor?" Confucius said, "A Jun Zi's top objective is righteousness. If a Jun Zi has valor but acts against righteousness, he is prone to make trouble. If a Xiao Ren has valor but acts against righteousness, he is prone to commit crimes."

23a Jun Zi (君子) is a gentleman, a person of noble character, a prominent and respectable person in society, or a person who upholds virtuous principles.

A Xiao Ren (小人) is a person with the opposite characteristics of a Jun Zi. A Xiao Ren is, for example, mean, wicked, cruel, dumb and/or lacking in virtues.

24 Zi Gong asked, "Does a Jun Zi hate anything?" Confucius said, "Yes, there are things he hates. He hates to disclose the faults of others. As a subordinate, he hates to slander his superiors. He hates people who are brave but do not follow Li. He hates determined but stubborn people." Confucius then asked, "Ci, do you hate anything?"

Zi Gong replied, "I hate people who plagiarize and pretend to be knowledgeable. I hate people who mistake immodesty as valor. I hate people who expose secrets of others to show their uprightness."

24a Zi Gong (子貢, also known as Duan Mu Ci端木賜, born around 520 BC) was one of the top ten disciples of Confucius. He later became the prime minister of the states of Lu (魯國) and Wey (衛國). He also made a fortune in business and was the wealthiest disciple of Confucius. He advocated making money through propriety, honesty, and trust. His eloquence was also well known. After Confucius's death, Zi Gong observed six years of mourning vigil to show his deep respect for Confucius.

25 Confucius said, "Women and Xiao Ren are difficult to please. If you are too close to them, they become spoiled. If you stay away from them, they complain."

26 Confucius said, "If a person has reached forty but is still an outcast, he will not have much hope for the rest of his life."

CHAPTER 18

WEI ZI (微子)

1 Wei Zi left the court. Ji Zi became a slave. Bi Gan died after giving good advice to the king. Confucius said, "The Yan Dynasty had three men with Ren virtue."

1a The Yan Dynasty (殷朝) was also called the Shang Dynasty (商朝) and was from about 1766 to 1046 BC.

Emperor Zhou (紂) was the last emperor of the Shang Dynasty. He was a notoriously brutal tyrant.

Wei Zi (微子) was Zhou's elder brother and was a viscount. Wei disagreed with Zhou on his brutality, quit the royal court, and retreated in the mountains.

Ji Zi (箕子) was an uncle of Emperor Zhou and his private tutor. Ji Zi repeatedly advised Zhou to stop his tyranny but failed to change him. Ji Zi then faked madness. Zhou then imprisoned and enslaved Ji Zi. After Zhou was defeated by King Wu (周武王) of the Zhou Dynasty (周朝), Ji Zi was eventually set free.

Bi Gan (比干) was also an uncle of Emperor Zhou and one of his tutors. Bi Gan also advised Zhou to stop his brutality. Bi Gan once wrote that being a counsel of the emperor, he had the responsibility to advise the emperor. He would rather die than keep his mouth shut. The enraged Zhou said to his other ministers, "I heard that a virtuous person's heart has seven holes. Let us verify whether Bi Gan's heart has seven holes." Zhou then ordered them to cut out Bi Gan's heart and show the other ministers that Bi Gan's heart did not have seven holes.

2 Liu Xia Hui was repeatedly fired as the chief justice. Some people asked him, "Why can't you go elsewhere?" He said, "Since I deal with people based on righteousness, which country would not fire me repeatedly? If I am required to bend my righteousness to serve my boss, why should I leave my motherland?"

2a Liu Xia Hui (柳下惠, 720–621 BC) was once an official of the state of Lu (魯國). He later resigned and became a hermit. He was fired many times as the chief justice (see chapter 14, paragraph 37).

3 Qi Jing Gong wanted to hire Confucius and said, "I cannot give him a position equivalent to Ji Si of the state of Lu. Perhaps I can put him in an equivalent position somewhere between Ji Si and Meng Si of the state of Lu." He then added, "I am too old already. I cannot hire him." Confucius then left the state of Qi.

3a Qi Jing Gong (齊景公) was the duke of Qi (齊國). According to historians, he was not a good king. He indulged in lavishness, pleasure, and lust, and he did not care about the welfare of his people.

The Ji Si family was a prominent and wealthy family in the state of Lu (魯國). Ji Kang Zi (季康子, died 468 BC) was a descendant of the family and the prime minister of the state of Lu (魯國) during the reign of Ai Gong (哀公) and was the most powerful official.

The next dominant families were Meng Sun Si (孟孫氏) and then Su Sun Si (叔孫氏). The three families dominated the government of the state of Lu (魯國).

4 The state of Qi sent a troupe of beautiful [and sexy] female dancers and singers. Ji Huan Zi [of the state of Lu] accepted the gift. He indulged in their entertainment so much that he did not attended the royal court meeting for three days. The disappointed Confucius then quit his official job and left the state of Lu.

4a The state of Qi (齊國) was bigger than the state of Lu (魯國). Ji Huan Zi (季桓子) was a descendant of the Ji Si family and a prime minister of the state of Lu (魯國).

5 A madman from Chu blocked the carriage of Confucius, singing aloud, "A phoenix indeed. A phoenix indeed. Why has your virtue deteriorated so much? Let bygones be bygones. There is still time to catch up and repent. Forget it! Forget it! All rulers are so corrupt that they are hopeless." Confucius came out from the carriage and wanted to talk to him. Since he left quickly, Confucius could not talk with him.

5a A phoenix was a sacred bird in the legend. It symbolizes a hero with supernatural power to conquer evil and save the world. In this context, Confucius was regarded as a phoenix.

The madman wanted to tell Confucius not to hang on to dirty political circles and instead to retire as a hermit.

6 Chang Zu and Jie Ni worked together in the field. Confucius and his students passed by. He sent Zi Lu to ask directions to cross the river. Chang Zu said, "Who is that person holding the reins in the carriage there?" Zi Lu replied, "He is Confucius." Chang Zu then asked, "Is he the Kong Qiu of Lu?" Zi Lu replied, "Yes." Chang Zu

said, "He should know the directions." Zi Lu then asked Jie Ni for directions. Jie Ni asked, "Who are you?" Zi Lu replied, "I am Zhong You." Jie Ni asked, "Are you a disciple of Kong Qiu?" Zi Lu replied, "Yes." Jie Ni then said, "There are turbulent waters and flooding rivers all over the country. Who can change and tame them? You follow a master who tries to avoid corrupt people. Why not follow a master who avoids the corrupt world?" Jie Ni immediately turned his back and plowed the soil. Zi Lu reported the encounter to Confucius who lamented with a sigh, "We cannot live with birds and wild animals. If we do not live with mankind, with whom can we live? If morality prevails in the world, there is no need for me to change it."

6a Chang Zu (長沮) and Jie Ni (桀溺) were two known hermits.

Kong Qiu (孔丘) was an alias and common name of Confucius.

Zi Lu (子路, 542–480 BC also known as Zhong You 仲由) was best known for his ability and success in statesmanship. He was noted for his valor and sense of justice.

7 Zi Lu followed Confucius and happened to fall behind. He met an old man carrying plowing tools and a walking stick. Zi Lu asked, "Have you seen my master?" The old man replied, "That person does not labor with his four limbs and cannot recognize five types of grains. How can he deserve to be a master?" After that, the old man continued to plow the soil with his tools. Zi Lu stood there and bowed. The old man then invited Zi Lu to stay overnight with his family. He treated Zi Lu with chicken and rice and introduced his two sons to Zi Lu. In the morning, Zi Lu told Confucius about the encounter. Confucius said, "He is a hermit." Confucius then sent Zi Lu to look for the old man, who had already left. Zi Lu said, "Not taking up an official post and serving the country is not righteous. Even the social order between young and old cannot be abolished. Likewise, how can the relationship between the ruler and

his officials be abolished? If one stays aloof to preserve his purity, he is disrupting the social order. A Jun Zi becomes a government official to practice righteousness. We already expect in advance that ideal morality may not prevail in the world."

8 The following are virtuous hermits in history: Bo Yi, Shu Qi, Yu Zhong, Yi Yi, Zhu Zhang, Liu Xia Hui, and Shao Lian. Confucius said, "Bo Yi and Shu Qi did not debase their will and disgrace their noble characters." Confucius elaborated further, "Liu Xia Hui and Shao Lian debased their will and disgraced their noble characters. However, their words conformed with social norms, and their actions reflected their careful considerations. Those were all their merits." He then continued, "Yu Zhong and Yi Yi talked boldly and preserved their own purity by relinquishing power. I am different from them. I do not predetermine what should or should not be done."

8a Bo Yi (伯夷) and Shu Qi (叔齊) were two princes of the last duke of the feudal state of Gu Zhu (孤竹國), during the Shang Dynasty (商朝, 1766–1046 BC). Bo Yi was the eldest brother and Shu Qi was the youngest. Before their father died, Shu Qi was nominated to be his successor. Shu Qi abdicated his throne to his eldest brother, Bo Yi, and stressed that the eldest son should be the successor to the throne according to tradition. Bo Yi refused to accept because of the respect of his father's wish. Both eventually renounced the throne and migrated to the territory of the state of Zhou (周). Later, King Wu of Zhou (周武王) raised an army to invade the Shang Dynasty. Both Bo Yi and Shu Qi knelt in front of King Wu's chariot and begged King Wu not to invade the Shang Dynasty. King Wu eventually conquered the Shang Dynasty and founded the Zhou Dynasty (周朝). Bo Yi and Shu Qi refused to be subjects of the Zhou Dynasty and eat its food. They moved to the mountains and starved to death. These two ancient characters were regarded by historians to be model Jun Zis who had the Ren virtue.

Yu Zhong (虞仲, also known as Zhong Yong, 仲雍) was the second son of King Tai (周太王) of the kingdom of Zhou and had three sons: Tai Bo (泰伯), Zhong Yong (仲雍), and Ji Li (季歷). The youngest son, Ji Li, had a son, Chong (昌), who was regarded the best candidate to be the future leader of the country. Tai Bo left the country with his younger brother Zhong Yong to give way to Ji Li. Because of this, King Tai designated Ji Li to be his successor so that Chong would eventually become the king of the country. Confucius praised Tai Bo and Yu Zhong for their concession of the throne.

Liu Xia Hui (柳下惠, 720–621 BC) was once an official of the state of Lu (魯國). He later resigned and became a hermit. He was fired three times as the chief justice. Somebody asked him why he did not find a job in another country. He replied, "Since I act properly all the time, which country would not fire me?" (see chapter 18, paragraph 2).

Little was known about Yi Yi (夷逸) and Shao Lian (少連).

Zhu Zhang (朱張) was another ancient hermit. Little was known about him.

9 The grand music master, Zhi, went to the state of Qi. Gan, the bandmaster of the second course of the meal went to the state of Chu. Liao, the bandmaster at the third course of the meal, went to the state of Cai. Que, the bandmaster of the fourth course of the meal, went to the state of Qin. Fang Shu, the drum master, moved to the banks of the Yellow River. Wu, the master of the castanets, went to the banks of the Han River. Yang, the assistant music master, and Xiang, the master of the stone percussion, went to the seaside.

9a A dinner of the royal family in the era of Confucius had four courses. Music was played during the dinner. Top-ranked musicians played during the first course. Second-tier musicians played during the second course and so on. The names of the musicians were Zhi (摯), Gan (干), Liao (繚), Que (缺), Fang Shu (方叔), Wu (武), Yang (陽), and Xiang (襄).

The state of Qi (齊國), the state of Chu (楚國), and the state of Qin (秦國) were three of the seven hegemons during the Spring-Autumn Period. The state of Cai (蔡國) was small.

10 Zhou Gong told his son Lu Gong, "A Jun Zi does not neglect his family and relatives and does not cause resentment among his ministers for lack of their mandates. Therefore, if senior and seasoned ministers have not made serious mistakes, do not fire them. Do not rely on one person for everything and expect perfection from him."

10a Zhou Gong was the short name of Zhou Gong Dan (周公旦), the brother of King Wu (周武王) of the Zhou Dynasty (周朝), and a famous prime minister and a founding father of the Zhou Dynasty. He was bestowed the territory of Lu (魯國), which later became the state of Lu (魯國). His son Bo Qin (伯禽), also known as Lu Gong (魯公), was the founder of the state of Lu (魯國).

11 The Zhou Dynasty had eight sages as its ministers: Bo Da, Bo Shi, Zhong Tu, Zhong Hu, Shu Ye, Shu Xia, Ji Sui, and Ji Gua.

11a Little was known about Bo Da (伯達), Bo Shi (伯適), Zhong Tu (仲突), Zhong Hu (仲忽), Shu Ye (叔夜), Shu Xia (叔夏), Ji Sui (季隨), and Ji Gua (季騧).

CHAPTER 19

ZI ZHANG (子張)

1 Zi Zhang said, "An elite scholar in public service should be prepared to sacrifice his life in a dangerous crisis, think of righteousness when presented with an opportunity for gain [in terms of money, power, or fame], think of reverence during a worship ritual, and think of sorrow during a mourning vigil. Such a person deserves to be a scholar."

1a Zi Zhang (子張, 503–447 BC) was a disciple of Confucius.

2 Zi Zhang said, "If a person upholds his own virtues but does not promote them so that others will emulate him, and believes in moral principles but not firmly, does it matter whether he exists or not?"

3 Disciples of Zi Xia asked Zi Zhang about how to make friends. Zi Zhang asked, "What did he say?" The disciples replied, "Zi Xia said, 'Befriend people who deserve to be your friends. Otherwise, reject them.'" Zi Zhang said, "This is different from what I have heard. A Jun Zi respects virtuous and capable people but can accept everyone. He values capable and virtuous people and sympathizes with lesser people. Since he is magnanimous, who can he not accept?

If he is not virtuous, others will automatically reject him. Does he need to reject others?"

3a Zi Xia (子夏, born 507 BC) was a disciple of Confucius and later became an official of the state of Wei (魏國).

4 Zi Xia said, "Even minor cleverness can be remarkably appealing. However, when it is applied broadly, there is a risk of messing up major undertakings. Therefore, a Jun Zi does not apply it."

4a Zi Xia (子夏, born 507 BC) was a disciple of Confucius and later became an official of the state of Wei (魏國).

5 Zi Xia said, "If you know every day what you still do not know, and you do not forget at the end of a month what you have learned during the month, you are indeed a serious learner."

5a Zi Xia (子夏, born 507 BC) was a disciple of Confucius and later became an official of the state of Wei (魏國).

6 Zi Xia said, "If you are extensively knowledgeable, dedicated firmly to your goals, thoroughly inquisitive, and capable of self-reflection of yourself versus your environment, you are on the path to Ren virtue."

6a Zi Xia (子夏, born 507 BC) was a disciple of Confucius and later became an official of the state of Wei (魏國).

7 Zi Xia said, "Hundreds of mechanics work in factories to accomplish their projects. A Jun Zi learns to attain high moral standards."

7a Zi Xia (子夏, born 507 BC) was a disciple of Confucius and later became an official of the state of Wei (魏國).

8 Zi Xia said, "A Xiao Ren always tries to cover up and find excuses for his faults."

8a Zi Xia (子夏, born 507 BC) was a disciple of Confucius and later became an official of the state of Wei (魏國).

9 Zi Xia said, "A Jun Zi shows three different demeanors. Looked at from a distance, he appears stern. When he is approached, he is mild. When he speaks, his words are firm and authoritative."

9a Zi Xia (子夏, born 507 BC) was a disciple of Confucius and later became an official of the state of Wei (魏國).

10 Zi Xia said, "A Jun Zi must obtain his people's trust before sending out orders to them. If not, his people will feel they are being dictated upon. He must obtain his emperor's (boss's) trust before he gives advice. If not, the emperor (boss) will reject the advice as slander."

10a Zi Xia (子夏, born 507 BC) was a disciple of Confucius and later became an official of the state of Wei (魏國).

11 Zi Xia said, "A person with great virtues will never transgress any regulatory (and social) boundaries, whereas a person with little virtues tends to trespass the limits."

11a Zi Xia (子夏, born 507 BC) was a disciple of Confucius and later became an official of the state of Wei (魏國).

12 Zi You criticized Zi Xia and said, "The disciples of Zi Xia just know how to sweep the floor and receive guests. These are just trivial. They have not been taught the core of learning yet." The upset Zi Xia said, "No, you are quite wrong. Regarding moral principles for a Jun Zi, what are the priorities and what are secondary? Take,

for example, the many kinds of plants. Which are more important than others? Regarding the moral principles for a Jun Zi, can you degrade any of them? Only great saints can accomplish all of them from the beginning to the end."

12a Zi You (子 游, also known as Yan Yan言偃, 506–443 BC) was a prominent disciple of Confucius.

Zi Xia (子夏, born 507 BC) was a disciple of Confucius and later became an official of the state of Wei (魏國).

13 Zi Xia said, "After a scholar in public service has fulfilled his duties, he should devote his leisure time to learning. After a scholar has learned enough, he should apply for an official job in public service."

13a Zi Xia (子夏, born 507 BC) was a disciple of Confucius and later became an official of the state of Wei (魏國).

14 Zi You said, "Mourning should stop at a feeling of grief and not beyond."

14a Zi You (子游, also known as Yan Yan, 言偃, 506–443 BC) was a prominent disciple of Confucius.

15 Zi You said, "My friend Zi Zhang is an outstanding person. However, he has not reached the standard of Ren virtue yet."

15a Zi You (子游, also known as Yan Yan, 言偃, 506–443 BC) was a prominent disciple of Confucius.

Zi Zhang (子張, 503–447 BC) was a disciple of Confucius.

16 Zheng Zi said, "Zi Zhang has elegant and imposing appearance. However, it is difficult to practice Ren virtues with him."

16a Zheng Zi (曾子, also known as Zheng Shen曾参, born 505 BC) was a prominent disciple of Confucius, known for his filial piety. He was the author of *The Book of Great Learning* (大學).

Zi Zhang (子張, 503–447 BC) was a disciple of Confucius.

17 Zheng Zi said, "I have heard from our master that people tend not to divulge their deep feelings. If they do, they must be mourning for their dead parents."

17a Zheng Zi (曾子, also known as Zheng Shen曾参, born 505 BC) was a prominent disciple of Confucius, known for his filial piety. He was the author of *The Book of Great Learning* (大學).

18 Zheng Zi said, "I have heard from our master that Meng Zhuang Zi was known for his filial piety, and others can emulate his filial piety in many respects, except that they will find it difficult not to change their father's ministers and policies."

18a Meng Zhuang Zi (孟莊子) was a minister of the state of Lu (魯國).

19 Meng Si appointed Yang Fu as the chief of criminal justice. Yang Fu consulted Zheng Zi about his new job. Zheng Zi said, "Since the rulers of the country have lost their moral and proper bearings, the people have degenerated for a long time. After you have uncovered the truth of your cases, you need to sympathize and pity the convicted. Don't feel proud of your ability to make judgment on the cases."

19a Meng Si (孟氏, also known as Meng Sun Si). The three dominant families of the state of Lu (魯國) were the descendants of Meng Sun Si (孟孫氏), Su Sun Si (叔孫氏), and Ji Sun Si (季孫氏). They dominated the court of the state of Lu.

Yang Fu (陽膚) was a disciple of Zheng Zi (曾子).

Zheng Zi (曾子, also known as Zheng Shen曾参, born 505 BC) was a prominent disciple of Confucius, known for his filial piety. He was the author of *The Book of Great Learning* (大學).

20 Zi Gong said, "Emperor Zhou's wickedness was not as much as what people think. Therefore, a Jun Zi dreads falling into an abyss of notoriety. Once there, everyone in the world will blame all evil on him."

20a Emperor Zhou (紂) was the last emperor of the Shang Dynasty. He was a notoriously brutal tyrant.

21 Zi Gong said, "The faults of a Jun Zi are like the eclipses of the sun and moon. When he has faults, everyone can see them. After he has corrected his faults, everyone will respect him."

22 Gong Sun Zhao of the state of Wey asked Zi Gong, "From whom did Zhong Ni [Confucius] get his education?" Zi Gong said, "The principles and doctrines laid down by King Wen and King Wu of the Zhou Dynasty have not fallen to the ground yet. They still prevail in society. Sages learn their central themes while lesser people learn their minor details. We can find such doctrines and principles everywhere. Where could my master not learn from? Why did he need to learn from only one teacher?"

22a Gong Sun Zhao (公孫朝) was a minister of the state of Wey (衛國).

Zhong Ni (仲尼) was an alias of Confucius.

Zi Gong (子貢, also known as Duan Mu Ci端木賜, born around 520 BC) was one of the top ten disciples of Confucius. He later became the prime minister of the states of Lu (魯國) and Wey (衛國). He also made a fortune in business and was the wealthiest disciple of Confucius. He advocated making money through propriety, honesty, and trust. His eloquence was also well known. After Confucius's death, Zi Gong observed six years of mourning vigil to show his deep respect for Confucius.

King Wen of the Zhou Dynasty (周文王, 1152–1056 BC), and King Wu of the Zhou Dynasty (周武王, died 1043 BC) are regarded by historians as saintly kings.

23 Shu Sun Wu Shu told other ministers in court, saying, "Zi Gong is more virtuous than Zhong Ni [Confucius]." Zi Fu Jing Bo related this comment to Zi Gong. Zi Gong said, "Let me use the walls of an estate as an analogy. The walls of my estate are only shoulder high. People can peep over it and see all the valuables in my house. My master's walls are several fathoms high. If one does not find the door and enter the estate, one cannot see the gorgeous temples and magnificent buildings inside the estate. It is a pity that very few people can find the door. It is understandable that Shu Sun Wu Shu has made that comment."

23a Shu Sun Wu Shu (叔孫武叔) was a minister of the state of Lu (魯國).

Zi Fu Jing Bo (子服景伯) was another minister of the state of Lu (魯國).

Zi Gong (子貢, also known as Duan Mu Ci 端木賜, born around 520 BC) was one of the top ten disciples of Confucius. He later became the prime minister of the states of Lu (魯國) and Wey (衛國). He also made a fortune in business and was the wealthiest disciple of Confucius. He advocated making money through propriety, honesty, and trust. His eloquence was also well known.

After Confucius's death, Zi Gong observed six years of mourning vigil to show his deep respect for Confucius.

Zhong Ni (仲尼) was an alias of Confucius.

24 Shu Sun Wu Shu reviled against Zhong Ni. Zi Gong said, "It is of no use doing so. Zhong Ni cannot be reviled. The virtues of other sages are like small mounds that can be stepped over easily. Zhong Ni is like the sun and the moon. How can one step over them? If one wants to get rid of the sun and moon by all means, what harm can he do to the sun and moon? This only shows his ineptness."

24a Shu Sun Wu Shu (叔孫武叔) was a minister of the state of Lu (魯國).

Zi Gong (子貢, also known as Duan Mu Ci端木賜, born around 520 BC) was one of the top ten disciples of Confucius. He later became the prime minister of the states of Lu (魯國) and Wey (衛國). He also made a fortune in business and was the wealthiest disciple of Confucius. He advocated making money through propriety, honesty, and trust. His eloquence was also well known. After Confucius's death, Zi Gong observed six years of mourning vigil to show his deep respect for Confucius.

Zhong Ni (仲尼) was an alias of Confucius.

25 Chen Zi Qin told Zi Gong, "You are too modest. How can Zhong Ni be more virtuous than you?" Zi Gong said, "One sentence uttered by a Jun Zi can show his wisdom, but one other sentence can show his stupidity. Therefore, one must be cautious with his words. The excellence of our master cannot be reached in the same way that no one can climb to the sky. If our master were appointed to head his country or his family, whatever he wanted to establish would be

accomplished. People would follow his leadership, be attracted by his benevolent policy, and respond positively to his encouragement. His life was glorious, and his death was a big pity. How can I measure up to him?"

25a Some scholars think Zi Qin (子禽, also known as Chen Kang 陈亢, born around 511 BC) was a student of Confucius, while others think he was not. He later became an official of the state of Wey (衛國).

Zi Gong (子貢, also known as Duan Mu Ci端木賜, born around 520 BC) was one of the top ten disciples of Confucius. He later became the prime minister of the states of Lu (魯國) and Wey (衛國). He also made a fortune in business and was the wealthiest disciple of Confucius. He advocated making money through propriety, honesty, and trust. His eloquence was also well known. After Confucius's death, Zi Gong observed six years of mourning vigil to show his deep respect for Confucius.

Zhong Ni (仲尼) was an alias of Confucius.

CHAPTER 20

YAO SAID (堯曰)

1 Yao said, "Oh! Shun! The divine mandate is now resting on your shoulders. Hold onto your call with sincerity and propriety. If poverty and suffering prevail in your country, which is surrounded by four seas, God's blessing on you will come to a perpetual end." Shun in turn delegated the same mandate to his successor, Yu.

Tang of the Shang Dynasty prayed, "May I, little Lu, venture to offer to You, O God, a black-skinned ox as a sacrifice. I sincerely pray to You that I dare not pardon my own sins. I, your humble servant, dare not hide from You since You are omniscient. If I have committed sins and offenses, I will not attribute them to my people. If my people have committed sins and offenses, they are all my fault."

The Zhou Dynasty conferred great gifts to people so that good people were enriched. However, there was a motto: "Even if one is related to the royal family, he does not have more privileges than virtuous persons. If my people have faults, the responsibility lies with me only." Zhou rulers carefully regulated and calibrated weights and measures, legislated laws and Li, restored discarded officials, and implemented a governance structure to all corners of the country. They also revived ruined states, restored families whose succession lines had been broken, and recruited hidden talents. They won the hearts of their people. Their top priorities were people, their food, their funerals, and their worship rituals. A benevolent policy won the hearts of the people. An honest policy won the trust of the people. Prompt devotion to work resulted in great achievements. By justice, all were delighted.

1a Ancient saintly kings refer to Yao (堯, 2356–2255 BC), Shun (舜, 2294–2184 BC), the Great Yu of Xia Dynasty (禹, around 2237–2139 BC), Tang of Shang Dynasty (湯, 1670–1587 BC), King Wen of the Zhou Dynasty (周文王, 1152–1056 BC), and King Wu of the Zhou Dynasty (周武王, died 1043 BC). During their regimes, ancient China had a near utopian society.

2 Zi Zhang asked Confucius, "How can I govern a country well?" Confucius said, "Observe five meritorious conducts and banish four evils. You can then rule a country well." Zi Zhang asked, "What do five meritorious conducts mean?" Confucius said, "A Jun Zi is beneficent but not wasteful, works hard without complaint, fulfills his needs without being covetous, is not arrogant and extravagant when he is wealthy, and is majestic but not fierce." Zi Zhang asked, "What does beneficent but not wasteful mean?" Confucius said, "If you provide your people with exactly what they need, are you not beneficent but not wasteful? If you assign the right people to work willingly, who will complain? If you want to have Ren virtue and get it, would you be greedy? A Jun Zi treats every group with due respect, irrespective of its size and power base. If you do so, would you not be wealthy but not arrogant and extravagant? A Jun Zi dresses decently and presents a dignified appearance so that people look at him with awe. If you do so, would you not be majestic but not fierce?" Zi Zhang asked, "What do four evils mean?" Confucius said, "If you do not educate your people before you implement capital punishment, you are brutal. If you do not give early warning but demand immediate results from people, you are oppressive. If you issue orders without urgency at first but later set time limits for

completion of projects, you are destructive. If you award or donate to people in a stingy way, you are just a mean miser."

2a Zi Zhang (子張, 503–447 BC) was a disciple of Confucius.

3 Confucius said, "If one does not know his fate and mission in life, he does not deserve to be a Jun Zi. If he does not know Li, he cannot establish himself in society. If he does not listen carefully and analytically, he cannot understand people."

3a The word *Li* (禮) in Confucianism and in the Chinese language in general has many meanings. In ancient times, it referred to rites, rituals in ceremonies, protocols in courts and government, discipline, regulations, laws and order, respect, courtesy, and etiquette in daily life; in modern times, it refers to respect, etiquette, courtesy, presents, and gifts. Li (禮) includes a set of social norms that are motivated by the inner conscience of people and entrenched in the culture rather than externally imposed by the government through decrees and legislation.

ENDNOTES

1   Zi (子) is a courteous address of "mister" or "master."

2   Jun Zi (君子) is used in Chinese scholarly texts to mean a gentleman, a person of superior and noble character, a prominent and respectable person in society, or a person who upholds high standards of virtuous principles. It was commonly translated as "gentleman" in the past, but as described throughout *The Analects*, a Jun Zi stands for a much wider range of excellence and a higher standard of morality than what the English word *gentleman* stands for. Therefore, this translation retains the transcribed term *Jun Zi* to preserve its authentic meaning in Chinese.

3   As explained throughout *The Analects*, the word *Ren* (仁) embodies all the core virtues of humanity, including love. This word was translated as "kindness" or "humaneness" in the past. Such an interpretation and translation of *Ren* does not convey the full meaning of the word in Chinese. There is no single word in English that encompasses all the meanings of the word in Chinese. Therefore, this translation uses the transcriptions of the Chinese word 仁 to preserve its authentic meanings.

4   *The Book of Great Learning* (大學) was one of the *Four Books* in Confucianism and a chapter of *The Book of Rites* (禮記). It was written by Zheng Zi (曾子). In the South Song Dynasty of China (1127–1279 AD), a prominent Confucian, Zhu Xi (朱熹), designated the Four Books—*The Book of Great Learning* (大學), *The Book of the Mean* (中庸, also known as The Doctrine of the Mean), *The Analects* (論語), and *Mencius* (孟子)—to be the required syllabus for the imperial examination for the recruitment to the civil service. This requirement lasted for the next three dynasties. The main theme of *The Book of Great Learning* was encapsulated in its

opening sentence: "The path of great learning is to be enlightened by Truth and to apply it to benefit people, and this path does not end until the ultimate excellence in virtue is achieved."

5   The Zhou Dynasty (周朝) was founded by King Wu (周武王) in 1066 BC. From 1066 to 770 (or 771) BC, this dynasty was called the Western Zhou Dynasty (西周) because its capital was located at Hao Jing (鎬京) in the west of China. After twelve successions of emperors, nomads from the west invaded the state, pillaged the capital, and killed King You (周幽王) of Zhou in 770 BC. His successor, King Ping (周平王), moved the capital eastward to Luoyi (雒邑, also known today as Luo Yang 洛陽 in Henan province 河南). This began the Eastern Zhou Dynasty (東周). Historians call the period from 771 to 476 BC the Spring-Autumn Period because Confucius wrote the *Spring-Autumn Annals*, a chronicle of the state of Lu (魯國) between 722 and 479 BC. The state of Lu was Confucius's motherland. During this period, the Zhou emperors, also called the imperial emperors (天子), lost effective authority over feudal states, which were de facto autonomous states. Dukes and feudal lords (諸侯) ruled their states as independent sovereigns with their own legislations, governments, armies, and taxations. These rulers of the feudal states paid homage to the imperial emperor only ceremonially. In this translation, the word *kings* is often used to describe such rulers rather than the word *dukes* because in the English tradition, dukes and noblemen had less independence from the monarch than the feudal rulers during the Spring-Autumn Period. Feudal rulers during the Spring-Autumn Period were effectively kings.

6   *The Book of Poetry* (詩經) is also translated as *The Book of Odes* or *The Chinese Classic of Poetry*. *The Book of History* is also translated as *The Book of Documents*. *The Book of Changes* is also called *The I Ching* (易經), which is directly transcribed from the Chinese name. Together with *The Book of Rites* and the *Spring-Autumn Annals*, the collection is known as *The Five Sutras*, *The Five Chinese Classics*, or *The Five Jings*. This translation uses the word *poetry* instead of *odes* because the former is more common in English.

7   *The Analects* mentioned the word *Li* (禮) many times. It is obvious from the messages in *The Analects* and from traditional usage of this word in Chinese culture that this word has many meanings. In ancient times, it

referred to rites, rituals, ceremonies, protocols in courts and government, discipline, regulations, laws and order, respect, courtesy, and etiquette in daily life; in modern times, it refers to respect, etiquette, courtesy, presents, and gifts. In general, Li (禮) includes a set of social norms that are motivated by the inner conscience of people and entrenched in the tradition and culture rather than externally imposed by the government through decrees and legislation. In some old translations, this word was translated as "rules of propriety." Such a translation was too narrow and ignored the ancient context as well as Chinese culture. Since no single English word can encapsulate all the meanings of Li (禮), this translation uses the transcription of the Chinese word to preserve the accuracy of the original text.

8   The word *De* or *Te* (德) in the Chinese language has many meanings. It is translated here as "moral and ethical principles." It is also translated as "inherent strength, integrity, deeds which follow the Way" in Taoism, "moral character, morality" in Confucianism, and "merit, virtuous deeds" in Buddhism.

9   A Xiao Ren (小人) is a person with the opposite characteristics of a Jun Zi. A Xiao Ren is, for example, mean, wicked, cruel, dumb, lacking of virtues, dishonest, low class, and so on. Some old translations used "mean man" to describe a Xiao Ren (小人). Since such a character has many inferior and obnoxious qualities, "mean man" is an incomplete description. There is no single English word that conveys all these qualities. To preserve the complete and accurate meaning of this phrase in Chinese culture, this translation therefore uses the transcription of the Chinese phrase.

10 The political map during the early part of the Spring-Autumn Period from 685 to 591 BC was dominated by five hegemons: the states of Qi (齊), Song (宋), Jin (晉), Qin (秦), and Chu (楚); or alternatively Qi (齊), Chu (楚), Jin (晉), Wu (吳), and Yue (越). Between 497 and 453 BC, the state of Jin broke up into three states: Han (韓), Zhao (趙), and Wei (魏). Therefore, during the second part of the Spring-Autumn Period from about 592 to 474 BC, there were seven hegemons: the states of Qi (齊), Chu (楚), Yue (越), Han (韓), Zhao (趙), Wei (魏), and Qin (秦) (see figure 1).

The state of Lu (魯國) was a small country from 1042 to 249 BC located around modern Shandong province in China. Its capital was Qufu (曲阜) where Confucius was born. The state of Lu was eventually dissolved into the state of Chu in about 250 BC. The ruler of the state of Lu during Confucius's time was Ai Gong (哀公). He was the twenty-sixth ruler of the state and the son of Ding Gong (定公). Confucius served Ding Gong as the chief of security and justice for a few years. The title of "Gong" was equivalent to a duke. Therefore, Ai Gong is also translated as "Duke Ai" by some translators. As explained in endnote 5, the translation in this book preserves the transcribed name from Chinese, since in English tradition, a duke has no sovereign power. Feudal rulers during the Spring-Autumn Period were de facto independent of the imperial emperor of the Zhou Dynasty and were literally kings. Therefore, the words *duke* and *king* are often used interchangeably in this translation.

11 "Guan Ju" (關雎) is the first poem of national folk songs (國風) in *The Book of Poetry* (詩經). This beautiful, romantic, and melancholic poem has been popular in China for millennia. It is difficult to communicate the beauty of this poem in a different language. The following translation attempts to give the reader a superficial flavor of it:

> A pair of "Ju" gulls are mating and quacking, "Guan, guan!"
> On the island in the river delta.
> A slender maiden over there is so modest and charming.
> I, a gentleman, yearn to marry her.
>
> That maiden is busy nipping,
> Tall and short stalks of vegetables.
> That slender and charming maiden,
> I dream of her day and night.
>
> My dream cannot come true.
> But I still think of her day and night.
> It hurts; it really hurts
> To roll in bed, unable to fall asleep.
>
> Tall and short stalks of vegetables on her sides,
> Are being nipped by her.
> That slender and charming maiden,
> I want to befriend her with harp music.

Long and short pieces of vegetables on her sides
Are being picked up by her.
That slender and charming maiden,
I want to lure her with bell and drum music.

12   *The Book of Filial Piety* is also known as *The Classic of Filial Piety* and *Xiao Jing* (孝經).

13   *Zuo Zhuan* (左傳) is also known as *The Zuo Tradition* or *The Commentary of Zuo*.

14   Zhong Yong (中庸) is also known as *The Doctrine of the Mean*. The word *Zhong* means "unbiased," "not in excess in one way or the other," and "nothing more and nothing less." The word *Yong* means "ordinary," "commonplace," "firm," "unwavering," and "perpetual truth." A prominent Confucian named Zhu Xi (朱熹) designated this book to be one of the Four Books:—*The Book of Great Learning* (大學), *The Book of the Mean* (中庸, also known as The Doctrine of the Mean), *The Analects* (論語), and *Mencius* (孟子)—to be the required syllabus for the imperial examination for the recruitment to the civil service. This requirement lasted for the next three dynasties. *The Doctrine of the Mean* implies moderation, objectivity, sincerity, and propriety. This book has three main themes: self-cultivation, leniency and forbearance, and sincerity.

15   *The Book of Changes* is also known as *The I Ching* (易經) and *The Classic of Changes*. This book originated in prehistorical times, the Fu Xi (伏羲) period in China, as a manual of divination and fortune-telling. It was further developed by King Wen (周文王) of Zhou. The manual gradually evolved into a book of wisdom about how the world changes and how a person should respond to those changes. Confucius wrote a commentary to the book developed by King Wu. The commentary consisted of ten chapters, called the *Ten Wings*. It focused more on philosophy than on fortune-telling. During the subsequent millennia, the theory of *The I Ching* about how events in the world change has been applied to many fields in China, including medicine, acupuncture, astrology, martial arts, art, building and architecture, tomb selection, military strategy, and technology. The interested reader can refer to reference 11 for further information.

REFERENCES

1. John Kirkly, Li Tianchen, *The Analects of Confucius: A Chinese-English Bilingual Translation* (Beijing: Zhonghua Book Company, 2002).

2. (a) D. C. Lau, *Tao Te Ching* (Hong Kong: Chinese University Press, 1989).
   (b) Victor H. Mair, ed., *Tao Te Ching: The Classic Book of Integrity and the Way* (New York: Bantam Books, 1990).
   (c) Wikipedia, s.v. "Tao Te Ching", last modified July 15, 2020, 21:59, http://en.wikipedia.org/wiki/Tao_Te_Ching.

3. (a) Wikipedia, s.v. "曾參", last modified May 15, 2020, 00:43, http://zh.wikipedia.org/wiki/曾參.
   (b) Wikipedia, s.v. "Zengzi", last modified May 2, 2020, 16:18, http://en.wikipedia.org/wiki/Zengzi.

4. Wikipedia, s.v. "大學", last modified August 1, 2020, 05:01, http://zh.wikipedia.org/wiki/大學.

5. Wikipedia, s.v. "Classic of Poetry", last modified July 7, 2020, 16:55, http://en.wikipedia.org/wiki/Classic_of_Poetry.

6. (a) Wikipedia, s.v. "Doctrine of the Mean", last modified July 17, 2020, 05:02, http://en.wikipedia.org/wiki/Doctrine_of_the_Mean.

(b) <u>Encyclopaedai</u> Britannica Online, s.v. "Zhongyong", last modified August 2, 2020, 14:10, https://www.britannica.com/topic/Zhongyong.

7. Wikipedia, s.v. "Spring and Autumn Period", last modified July 25, 2020, 16:39, http://en.wikipedia.org/wiki/Spring_and_Autumn_period.

8. Wikipedia, s.v. "Book of Documents", last modified July 17, 2020, 12:23, http://en.wikipedia.org/wiki/Book_of_Documents.

9. Ivan Chen, *The Book of Filial Piety* (London: J. Murray, 1908).

10. Wikipedia, s.v. "Doctrine of the Mean", last modified July 17, 2020, 05:02, http://en.wikipedia.org/wiki/Doctrine_of_the_Mean.

11. (a) Richard J. Lynn, The Classics of Changes (New York: Columbia University Press, 1994).
(b) Wikipedia, s.v. "I Ching", last modified July 17, 2020, 22:51, http://en.wikipedia.org/wiki/I_Ching.
(c) Richard J. Smith, The I Ching: A Biography (Princeton, NJ: Princeton University Press, 2012).
(d) Hellmut Wilhelm and Richard, Wilhelm, Understanding the I Ching (Princeton, NJ: Princeton University Press, 1995).

MAP

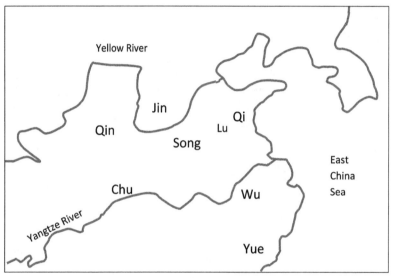

Fig. 1 Hegemons in Spring-Autumn Period

INDEX

CPSIA information can be obtained
at www.ICGtesting.com
Printed in the USA
BVHW042307141120
593269BV00011B/122